MW01502576

BUILDING THE HOME

BY LARRY ARROWOOD

BUILDING THE HOME

Biblical Blueprints for a Successful Marriage

Building the Home

by Larry Arrowood

©1991 Word Aflame Press
   Hazelwood, MO 63042-2299

Cover design by Tim Agnew

All Scripture quotations in this book are from the King James Version of the Bible unless otherwise identified.

All rights reserved. No portion of this publication may be reproduced, stored in an electronic system, or transmitted in any form or by any means, electronic, mechanical, photocopy, recording, or otherwise, without the prior permission of Word Aflame Press. Brief quotations may be used in literary reviews.

Printed in United States of America.

Printed by

Library of Congress Cataloging-in-Publication Data

Arrowood, Larry M., 1950–
        Building the home / Larry Arrowood.
              p.   cm.
        Includes bibliographical references.
        ISBN 0-932581-80-3
        1. Family—Religious life. 2. Marriage—Religious aspects—
Christianity. I. Title.
        BV4526.2.A74   1991
        248.4—dc20   90-29298
                                                           CIP

*To my wife, Nancy,
and sons, Andrew and Aaron,
who have joined me in building
the most loving place I know—
my home.*

Contents

Acknowledgements

With gratitude I acknowledge the following wonderful people who helped make this book possible: my wife, Nancy, for working with me through every chapter; Susan Henderson, for her dedication in compiling the final copy; Cassey Benanzer, Tammy Fisher, Margie McNall, and Sherry Smith for their many hours of typing; Zelma Sue Croucher for her poem; Mary Wallace for her insightful sharing on the subject; Tim Agnew for his cover design; David K. Bernard for his suggestions and final editing; and J. O. Wallace and the Word Aflame Press staff for the completed work.

Introduction

The Master Designer's keen eye saw that it was not good for man to be alone, so God created woman. This was the beginning of the oldest and most durable of all institutions, marriage. It is the basic structure of society even today.

Only two chapters into the Bible, we find God's ordaining of marriage: "Therefore shall a man leave his father and his mother, and shall cleave unto his wife: and they shall be one flesh" (Genesis 2:24). It is this union that Christ uses to describe His relationship with the church: "And there came unto me one of the seven angels . . . and talked with me, saying, Come hither, I will shew thee the bride, the Lamb's wife" (Revelation 21:9).

In an age when almost every worthwhile value is being tried, marriage and the home have come under serious attack. Divorce is no longer limited to the young and restless; it touches the lives of all ages. Grandchildren are now experiencing the trauma of seeing Grandma and Grandpa split up. The home is in serious trouble. Some doubt that it can survive. Fritz Ridenour writes, "That one permanent bastion of security and 'till death do us part' commitment has become for too many an impermanent gamble lasting till divorce seems convenient."[1] "Is

11

marriage, like the dinosaur, doomed to extinction?" asks Lawrence Van Gelder. "Or is it, at the very least, a candidate for formal evolution?"[2]

While some predict the collapse of the traditional family, others offer unconventional as well as unbiblical solutions. Judith Younger of Cornell University advocates a three-step plan for marriage. The first step would be a dress rehearsal that would require no license, carry no economic consequences, and have no legal obligations. No children would be permitted in this first stage. Although Ms. Younger's first step may sound practical for today's society, it would mandate an acceptance of fornication. Step two, selfish marriage, would carry more serious economic obligations but still would not involve child bearing. If a couple wanted to have children, they would engage in step three, marriage for children. This would require a written commitment to remain married until the children reached age eighteen.

Many such solutions have been offered, but none can replace that very practical, down-to-earth manual—the Bible. It strongly contends that marriage is for a lifetime. And to fulfill this lifetime commitment, the Bible offers guidelines to maintain the marriage. To veer from these guidelines will bring serious consequences and reduce a blissful home to a mere house, an expensive structure of wood, stone, and misery.

The chapters ahead will discuss many pitfalls that can destroy a family but will also give many suggestions to help make a home the most pleasant place in the world. How wonderful it is when a husband, wife, or child looks at a watch and exclaims joyfully, "It's time to go home!"

Our home can be our haven on earth. As Don Luftig

states, however, "Building a good marriage has never been easy and many people give up too soon."[3] It will take much effort on our part, but the benefits are priceless.

Are you interested in building a home? Then continue reading for twelve chapters about family building. The chapters ahead compare the building of a house and the building of a home. This analogy has been chosen because too many people put forth great effort to establish a physical structure but overlook what is most important, the family structure. A house can be built in six to eight weeks. In a few decades, it will deteriorate and be torn down. Building a home takes a lifetime, but its rewards are eternal.

1

Selecting a Blueprint

"*B*eautiful houses! 120 architect-designed houses to choose from. One-story, two-story, or multi-level plans with designs for all budgets. Floor space ranges from 1,248 to 4,448 square feet in your favorite early American, contemporary, Tudor, French, or Spanish style."

These words sound familiar to anyone who has seriously considered building a house. They are an advertisement for blueprints of houses. Someone can easily pick up the telephone and place an order for the blueprint of his choice.

A blueprint contains everything needed to build a house, including room dimensions, cooking and heating locations, electrical plans, and plumbing plans. What a marvelous invention, the blueprint! It shows in minute detail what the finished house will be like.

But if we go through all the bother to plan for a house, shouldn't we give serious consideration to how we will live in the house and with whom? We can draw an interesting and instructive analogy between a blueprint for a house and the planning for a marriage.

The Need

The first rule in selecting a blueprint for a house is to determine the needs of the family that will live in the house. Should there be three bedrooms or four? Is there need for a formal dining room for entertaining or a workshop for the handyman? Likewise, before marriage vows are exchanged, the needs of both partners must be thoroughly considered.

Let's determine the reasons for marrying. Is it companionship? Love? Security? The motives are important to the success of a marriage.

What does a prospective partner expect financially? George married Beth because he felt she would inherit a large sum of money and they would live happily without toil. That was twenty years ago, but her parents are still alive, and financial security has not materialized. A strain has developed on their vow "for richer or poorer."

Does a prospective mate want a large family or no children? What are the emotional needs of a prospective mate? Will she be able to accept sixty-hour work weeks for the striving young executive? Can he cope with her working and completing college, or will he feel deprived and cheated? Does she desire the fulfillment of an outside job that uses her mental ability and training? Does he want a wife who is there with supper on the table when he arrives home? These questions should be answered before the wedding date is set, or better yet, before a proposal is made or accepted.

Goals

In selecting a blueprint for a house, a couple should compare their goals. If they expect to move in five years, the resale value and demand for the house are essential considerations. If they expect a longer stay, maintenance-free materials and extras are justified.

When two people are united in marriage, they bring together many goals, both short-range and long-range. Heavy disagreements and sometimes divorce result from conflicting goals or expectations. Regina left Bill when he began his ministry in another state. She did not want to live that far from her parents, and most of all she just did not want to be married to a preacher. It certainly would have been better had they thoroughly discussed these feelings prior to marriage. Some goals may have to be abandoned and others adopted to have a harmonious marriage. Some compromises can cause bitterness and resentment to surface later in life.

For Christians, the ultimate long-range goal is heaven. Short-range goals need to work toward this end. Daily devotion and service to Christ are necessary. A couple should discuss their spiritual goals. They must allow time for personal Christian service, teaching a Sunday school class, choir practice, or ladies auxiliary work. Some will need to agree on which Apostolic church to attend—his or hers.

Financially, how is success spelled? P-a-y-c-h-e-c-k or s-a-v-i-n-g-s? Long-range goals are accomplished by reaching short-range goals step by step. The couple should be willing to make small sacrifices now to continue needed education and to save for future financial security. It is easy to want to lose twenty pounds, but this can't be accomplished without putting forth the effort to lose the first pound. If a woman needs a new outfit each week or otherwise spends her money foolishly, the wedding vows may not change her. Similarly, some men feel they need flashy cars or expensive hobbies. The couple should determine joint financial goals before marriage and work at them consistently.

Each mate should be willing and able to accept the other's career choice. A young mechanic does not want a wife who is embarrassed by what she considers the indignity of his trade. Similarly, someone simply cannot dress stylishly all the time and run a pig farm. Some professions require city living or frequent moves.

Bill, a company executive, moved with his new bride to Seattle. About a year later he received a call from corporate headquarters. "Say, Bill, we're giving you a promotion. We're not sure where, but pack up, take a week's vacation, and meet us in New York. We'll let you know when you arrive." Later he was asked to move from New York to Memphis, from Memphis to Colorado. Each move lasted about one and a half years. Each time his wife found a new job. The move to Colorado was to last at least five years, plenty of time to buy a house and settle down. Just over a year later, however, Bill and his wife were asked to pack again. Bill describes his wife, "She's the greatest to put up with my career."

It is imperative that the husband and wife be in agreement on such a career. Their goals should be compatible and not clash like plaids and stripes. "But we are in love," some protest, arguing that these considerations do not matter. Nevertheless conflicting goals can adversely affect a love relationship.

Though goal compromises are often necessary, some can be very unfair. A humorous tale illustrates this point well. A man went hunting to kill a bear and make himself a fur coat. He met a bear that was also hunting, looking for a nice meal. As the man took aim at the bear, he was momentarily stunned by the bear's suggestion. "Hold on a minute. Can't we talk about this? Perhaps we can reach an agreement." And so they sat down on a log to discuss the situation. By and by, the discussion ended with a compromise. The bear was able to have his morning meal. And the hunter? Well, he was wearing his fur coat.

Serious consideration should be given to the lasting effects of goal compromise. The wedding vows are an acknowledgement of acceptance of each other as we are rather than what we expect each to become through a series of bargaining compromises.

Here is a simple test to help determine if goals are compatible.

Test for the Man

1. Is she serious about her walk with God? An evaluation of her prayer life, worship, and church involvement can help answer this question.
2. Does she dress modestly and conduct herself in a Christian manner in public and in private?
3. Does she spend her money wisely?
4. Will she be a good homemaker? How she helps with household duties in her parents' home is indicative.
5. What are her special interests or hobbies? Do they hold interest for you, or can you at least accept them?

19

Test for the Woman

1. Is he serious about his walk with God? An evaluation of his prayer life, worship, and church involvement can help answer this question.
2. Does he treat you respectfully both in public and in private?
3. Does he presently have a good job?
4. Are his job changes necessary, and are they promotions?
5. Does he spend his money wisely?
6. Does he tithe and give liberally to the work of the Lord?
7. What are his special interests or hobbies? Do they hold interest for you, or can you at least accept them?

Let's look more closely at some of the questions. *Is he/she serious about his/her walk with God?* A church wedding doesn't bring spirituality into a home. This commitment must already be present. After marriage a person is less inclined to change a lifestyle in order to please a mate. Psychologically, the person feels that he has already won the war. The "principle of least interest" is at work here: the person least interested has the greater power. A person's interest in attracting a mate is greater before the wedding; if he did not become spiritually minded then, he most likely will not do so after the wedding vows.

Does he treat you respectfully both in public and in private? Or does he (or she, for that matter) try to persuade you to compromise your convictions? A Christian should not want anyone to do anything that causes guilt or destroys dedication. It may begin as a request to attend a "Christian" movie, but then become a request to attend a regular movie, and then one at a more offensive rating and then. . . . If one person puts on a good show in public but does not uphold that position privately, the marriage will be likely to fail in the private arena.

We are often shocked by the horrible stories of wife abuse. A recent study sheds light on the root of this problem: It is often a mere carryover of dating habits. A survey among students at Arizona State University revealed that sixty percent of those surveyed experienced some form of violence during courtship.[1] A young lady who is beaten or raped by her boyfriend often accepts his invitation for marriage. A study of 369 engaged couples found that thirty-four percent of the men had physically assaulted their fiancees at least once.[2] The man advances from girlfriend abuser to fiancee abuser to wife abuser. If temper tantrums and lack of self-control are present before marriage, the unacceptable behavior will only magnify after vows are exchanged. Promises to change later are promises of heartache for the mate.

Does he have a good job? Inconsistency in keeping employment may be a sign of immaturity and also laziness. A person tends to follow the same lifestyle patterns even after marriage. Yes, some men do mature with time, but is the wife willing to be the breadwinner while the "baby" grows up? If someone constantly changes jobs without an extremely good reason, his record will soon catch up with him.

Does he/she spend his/her money wisely? Can the couple afford the expensive habits of one partner? These will probably become demands after marriage. For example, Gary has been forced to work two full-time jobs for fifteen years to pay for his wife's excessive desires, and no change is in sight.

Does he tithe? God's blessings rest upon good stewardship. Moreover, if someone is selfish in giving to the work of the Lord, very possibly he will be selfish with his spouse. Unfaithfulness in tithing may also stem from lack of discipline, which carries over into other areas of life such as paying bills, keeping commitments, job responsibilities, and so on.

Will she be a good homemaker? If the bride-to-be does not presently help with the responsibilities at home, the future husband may be left with the choice of accepting an unkempt home or cleaning it himself, eating frozen dinners or fix-it-yourself meals. What kind of mother will such a person be to the children?

What are his/her special interests or hobbies? Individual interests can draw a couple together or take them in separate directions. What does the husband do if he loves camping but his wife panics at the sight of a cricket? What if a woman longs to skydive but her husband gets dizzy on a ladder? While each partner may enjoy and participate in some activities that the other does not, a couple should cultivate some activities that they can enjoy doing together.

If your answers to the foregoing questions keep turning up no, you need to do some serious talking with your future spouse. Can you accept each other as you are now "till death do us part"? Don't wait until after the ceremony to find out that the two of you can't live happily under the same roof. If necessary, let the battle rage before the marriage. After the smoke clears, and if you are willing to make a mutually agreeable compromise, go ahead and send out the invitations.

Style

The style of any house is important to those who live in it. The wife may like a convenient layout of the kitchen with an adjoining family room. The husband may appreciate an upstairs study off the master bedroom.

Likewise, personality or social style is a very important factor in selecting a spouse. In recent years, much has been written concerning individual personality types. Authors refer to them with different terms, but all agree that the human race is made up of different personalities with certain distinguishable qualities and drawbacks. They have also determined that certain personalities tend to be more compatible.

Marriage does not eliminate personality conflicts. The extrovert may want to entertain incessantly while the introverted mate pleads for time alone to sit by the fireplace with a good book. A highly assertive person may have an overwhelming effect on an unassertive spouse. On the other hand, two highly assertive persons may fight like cats with their tails tied together. An unresponsive person may drive a talkative spouse up the wall or vice versa. Marriage can be the melting pot of different styles so long as the heat produced by unwanted friction does not reach the boiling point.

Here is a rule of thumb concerning social style and marriage: If a dating couple cannot get along, they should not consider marriage a cure-all. If arguments persist before marriage, they will probably escalate after the wedding. Personality differences that irk now will probably remain irksome. Can a time-conscious, punctual husband endure a never-in-a-hurry-always-thirty-minutes-late wife? This question may seem trivial until the husband discovers that she is thirty minutes late for everything, including an important business appointment. How does elegant Ellen endure haphazard Harry? Does she mind muddy shoes trudged across the shiny kitchen floor?

No one likes to change. All want to be accepted "as is." Before marriage, then, the partners must decide to accept each other with all their traits and flaws and not let them become sources of continual conflict.

Cost

We don't waste time purchasing blueprints on a house that our budget has already dictated we cannot afford. Blueprints are designed for different incomes. It is wise to select an affordable house plan from the start. Jesus commented about the importance of finance as a factor in decision making: "For which of you, intending to build a tower, sitteth not down first, and counteth the cost, whether he have sufficient to finish it? Lest haply, after he hath laid the foundation, and is not able to finish it, all that behold it begin to mock him, saying, This man began to build, and was not able to finish" (Luke 14:28-30). Likewise, financial considerations must be included in marriage plans.

All too often, men view marriage as a means of dividing their expenses. But marriage tends to add expense, not divide it. The anticipated initial saving soon vanishes with reality.

It is scriptural for a man to provide financially for his family. "But if any provide not for his own, and specially for those of his own house, he hath denied the faith, and is worse than an infidel" (I Timothy 5:8). Without question, financial obligations are primarily the husband's responsibility.

Of course, the wife can help financially. Proverbs 31 praises the industry of the virtuous woman. "She considereth a field, and buyeth it: with the fruit of her hands she planteth a vineyard. . . . She maketh fine linen, and selleth it; and delivereth girdles unto the merchant" (Proverbs 31:16, 24).

Many couples fail to discuss seriously their finances prior to marriage. But financial planning should be an open and integral part of the marriage plans.

Since the husband is primarily responsible for supporting the home, here are some simple questions to help determine his present ability to do so.

1. Do you make enough money to support two? Three?

2. Do you presently have a savings account?

3. Are you prepared for any immediate cost-of-living increases or emergencies?

4. Will you and your bride be able to pay for the wedding without borrowing money?

5. Do you have, or are you presently working towards, the proper education for advancement in your chosen career?

6. Do you have adequate health and life insurance, including maternity insurance?

7. Could you put your immediate paycheck in the bank and not be faced with a past-due bill?

A negative answer to any one of these questions is an indication that the man's financial planning is insufficient. According to statistics, more domestic problems result from financial difficulties than from any other single cause. Couples should sit down and discuss their budget realistically.

A young friend selected an expensive apartment to impress his new bride. The honeymoon ended abruptly when they faced legal complications for breaking their lease and moving into an apartment that they could afford. His bride confided, "I wish he would have talked with me about it. I didn't care about the apartment. I just wanted to be with him." It is important to plan a reasonable budget together and then stick to the plan.

Today's economy forces many women into the work force, although some women work primarily to meet personal goals or to provide a higher (but not strictly necessary) standard of living. In 1984, more than two-thirds of American women ages twenty-five to fifty-four were working outside the home. Early in marriage, a second income offers a good opportunity to save for a down payment on a house or a memorable vacation.

There are two problems in planning a wife's income into the budget, however. First, there is the unplanned pregnancy. Some women have complications in pregnancy that make it impossible for them to hold down a job or at least to return to work immediately.

Second, double demands are typically placed upon the working wife. Many men are not willing to share equally the responsibilities in the home with the working wife. A recent survey found that sixty percent of men in a two-earner household do less than one-fourth of the housework.[3] Most working wives basically hold down two full-time jobs, and there is no substantial change in sight. Out of frustration and overwork, a wife may decide to quit her job and become a full-time homemaker.

For these reasons, the second income may no longer be available. Consequently, a second income should be

26

used for savings or for purchases above and beyond normal living expenses.

The ideal financial plan permits the wife to quit work when children come and to dedicate herself to the care, Christian training, and development of the children, particularly in their early years. The mother may want to reenter the public work force later. If out of necessity she must work, the parents should make diligent efforts to select a proper sitter or child-care facility.

In selecting a blueprint for marriage, couples should consider these four areas: needs, goals, style, and cost. Only after an honest, thorough evaluation of these matters are they ready to proceed to the next area of building.

2

Communication

*M*usic is written in a universal language. A musician can select music written by a Frenchman, American, or Italian and still be able to play it. Blueprints are designed in a similar manner. Masons, plumbers, electricians, and carpenters all read the same set of blueprints. They all understand the various markings on the blueprint. Each trade can see how its individual work fits into the whole.

Such communication is essential to the completion of a well-built house. Interruption of the communication process stopped the Tower of Babel building program. When builders could no longer communicate, the work ceased. Saw and hammer were silenced as builders went separate ways.

Communication is also vital in building a home. Breakdown in communication sends the family members in separate directions. Chapter 1 has explained the importance of understanding one another's needs, agreeing on goals, and working together to build our homes.

Communication is the vehicle for making these ideas known, and successful communication involves four areas: talking, listening, understanding, and honesty.

Talking

In the Garden of Eden in the cool of the day God walked and talked with Adam. God could read Adam's mind, but He chose to communicate audibly with him. Why? For real communication to take place, both parties must understand the thoughts and ideas of the other. Adam could not read God's mind; therefore, God communicated with him verbally. God established talking as part of the communication process.

Humans are born with all the essential components to transmit and receive ideas—a mind, a mouth, and two ears. How well these components are used is up to the individual. Good communication is not an innate ability. It is developed.

Some mistake the chatterbox for a good communicator. We sometimes speak of "the gift of gab." After listening to some of these so-called gifted people, however, we sometimes wonder, What are they really saying? Often the answer is, Nothing worthwhile. Someone once said: "Wise men speak because they have something to say; fools speak because they have to say something."

One researcher suggests that communication consists of a combination of ingredients: seven percent verbal, thirty-eight percent vocal, and fifty-five percent facial expression.[1] While some confuse incessant talking with communication, others feel that if they listen well then they are good communicators. This is true if they offer sufficient feedback to the talker by such means as verbal, vocal, and facial expressions.

Though words can become monotonous, the Bible underscores the value of well-chosen words. "A word fitly spoken is like apples of gold in pictures of silver" (Proverbs 25:11). "Pleasant words are as an honeycomb, sweet to the soul, and health to the bones" (Proverbs 16:24). "The Lord GOD hath given me the tongue of the learned, that I should know how to speak a word in season to him that is weary" (Isaiah 50:4).

Listening and Understanding

An interesting story is told about a boy named Bobby who grew up in a small town in Ohio. Though mentally disabled, Bobby loved to talk and was a friend to everyone in town. He liked being helpful and important. Bobby would select an intersection, stand in the middle of the street, and direct traffic. Everyone played along with the game. On one occasion, Bobby decided to record all the license numbers of cars he determined were speeding. The sheriff knew Bobby personally and allowed him telephone time to read his list of violators, playing along by responding with ummms and ahhhhs in appropriate places. Bobby caught him off guard when he concluded, "Now, Sheriff, read those numbers back to me, and let's see if you have them all right." The sheriff was caught. He had paid little attention to the numbers. Real communication was not taking place.

We are all guilty of failing to listen. We learn how to appear to be listening while our minds are a million miles away. A gibe was made regarding one of our previous presidents: "I know you believe you understand what you think I said, but I'm not sure you realize that what you heard is not what I meant." This saying is typical of the communication habits of many people.

31

A telephone in proper working order is equipped for both receiving and transmitting. Both functions are necessary for successful communication. But these alone are not enough. Understanding must also accompany the exchange. Too often our conversations sound like what Dr. Paul Tournier termed as "dialogues of the deaf."[2] Words are spoken, but none are comprehended.

Some conversations resemble a debate. Each person listens only for the sake of establishing his argument or for what I call the "topper story." A factory worker, nicknamed Topper by his fellow workmen, when hearing about another worker's experience, no matter how fantastic, would always respond, "That's nothing. Wait till you hear this one." He did not try to genuinely understand and appreciate what the other person was saying or feeling.

Here's a typical conversation between a husband and wife.

Wife: "The flower show was absolutely beautiful today."

Husband: "Hmmm . . . is that right? I'm considering trading in our old car on a prettier, more economical model."

Wife: "I especially liked the roses. They reminded me of the time you sent roses to me on our anniversary."

Husband: "Uh huh. I saw a rose-colored car today I really liked. I think I'll test-drive it tomorrow."

Both are talking and, to a degree, they are hearing, but neither is really communicating. There is no sharing of consistent ideas or thoughts. The words are vibrating the eardrums but not really registering in the conscious mind—at best they are only perpetuating the hearer's own thoughts.

Denis Waitley explains how this lack of communication can occur:

Radiating from your brain stem is a small network of cells, about four inches in length, called the "reticular activating system." It is just about the size and shape of a quarter of an apple. I like to refer to it as your own built-in "Apple" computer. The reticular activating system performs the unique function of filtering incoming sensory stimuli (sight, sound, smell, and touch) and determining which ones are going to become part of your world.[3]

Too often we use this system to filter out the communication attempts of our family. The wife may notice what is happening and think to herself, He isn't interested in anything I am saying. Actually both may have withheld their full attention.

We can also be guilty of this lack of communication with our children. A mother may become frustrated because her ten-year-old begins each statement with a toy-gun staccato: "Mom, mom, mom, mom, mom." Mother scolds the child when, in reality, it was learned behavior on the child's part. That was the only way he could get Mom's full attention. The thoughts and ideas of a child may seem unimportant to everyone except the child. Our responses, or lack of them, can help or hinder the child's self-esteem.

We too soon forget how thrilled we were with our child's first faltering sounds. We encouraged that little one to talk, and we listened raptly. Why now do we attempt to stifle our child's expression of himself by our refusal to listen? Children need communication. The average American parent must be oblivious to this fact, because, according to one estimate, as little as seven minutes a week are spent between child and parent in genuine communication.

Our indifference may not seem serious the first time or two it happens, but it can become a wedge in a family's communication ability. Misunderstandings occur when, due to the lack of real communication, members must surmise what the others are thinking. We can take the following steps to prevent this problem.

1. Take time to talk to your spouse and children every day.

2. Become a good listener by being genuinely interested in what they are saying.

3. Really think about what is being said.

4. Try to understand how the other person feels.

5. Respect the other person's feelings.

Communication does not mean agreeing all the time. It is an art to be able to disagree agreeably. As the French philosopher Voltaire stated, "I disapprove of what you say, but I will defend to the death your right to say it."

For example, women do not so much want to be right as they want to be understood. "Do you see *why* I have hurt feelings?" a wife may ask. The smart husband tries to understand the tender feelings of his wife and not judge her by his own feelings. When the Bible speaks of a woman being the "weaker vessel" (I Peter 3:7), it does not mean weaker in terms of stamina. Too many strong, dedicated women have proven that idea false. It refers to their sensitive emotional nature, which can be easily bruised or hurt by the thoughtlessness of their husbands.

Communication is not more important to women than it is to men, but the type of communication both sexes need is sometimes different. For example, Carol forced her husband to share his feelings with other men because she showed no interest in his thrill at catching the eight-pound bass. To have total communication, both marriage partners must try to understand the communication needs of the other.

Honesty

In this section we will deal not so much with truth and falsehood as with openness and completeness. A degree of dishonesty lies in failing to tell all the facts or in using certain voice inflections to destroy the truth. The Lord was well aware of the actions of Adam and Eve when they ate of the forbidden fruit, yet God asked Adam, in essence, "Why are you hiding?" He gave Adam an opportunity to communicate honestly about his disobedience, admit guilt, and ask for forgiveness.

Why do some people find it extremely difficult to be completely open and honest? A major reason is fear of rejection. They reason, Maybe my spouse won't think as highly of me if he or she knows my faults. My parents will be disappointed in me. But a life of pretense is very lonely. Burdens shared are burdens lightened.

Does every mistake made need to be dug up and exposed? No. We should use discretion in any decision to disclose the past, though sometimes confession is necessary for spiritual growth and emotional well-being. At other times, however, confession would only bring unnecessary pain to a spouse. But there are many here-and-now situations, circumstances, and happenings that

35

bother us. We can share our feelings of insecurity, loneliness, and disappointment. It is cruel to drop a bombshell ten years later and say, "I always hated those red roses you sent me every birthday. I really wanted pink carnations, but I was afraid if I told you, you would be upset."

Here is a list of rules to aid communication skills in the home:

1. *A decision that affects more than one person should be discussed with all members involved.* Example: The husband is offered a job promotion, and the promotion requires relocating. His decision to accept will affect the entire family. The children must change schools and make new friends. The wife will be further away from her elderly, sick parents. She will have to find another job. The family will have to select and adjust to a new church home. The promotion could mean that the husband will be away from home for extra hours. How will that affect home life and time now spent together? Can the children cope with such a change? Although the children must accept the decision of the parents, they should be allowed to share their feelings. They must be assured of the advantages of the move. The attitude of "We're moving whether you like it or not" is unwise, and it may lead to the heartache of rebellious children.

2. *Communicate in a kind tone.* "Impossible!" some say. Admittedly, some will have to unlearn a few bad habits, but the rewards of kind communication far outweigh the efforts. Speaking in loud or harsh tones places a spouse or children on the defensive. They often respond in the same manner. Proverbs 15:1 teaches, "A soft answer turneth away wrath: but grievous words stir

up anger." The Bible also warns, "Fathers, provoke not your children to anger, lest they be discouraged" (Colossians 3:21). Contrary to common parental practices, sound technicians suggest that people listen to a quiet tone more intently than a loud tone.

Loudness has adverse effects on us emotionally. It brings out the fight/flight instinct in us. There are times when parents must speak firmly with their children. If yelling is the constant means of communication, however, it loses its effect. For example, John, a young father, assumes that yelling is for correction, but because he yells constantly his four-year-old has learned to ignore even the yelling.

3. *Communicate affection.* People need to know they are loved and appreciated. We are often too busy to take time to express affection. "Have you hugged your child today?" glares accusingly at us from a bumper sticker. Jesus took the little children "up in his arms, put his hands upon them, and blessed them" (Mark 10:16). Jesus displayed affection for little children by touching them. We must not deny our families the assurance of our love. The wife should not have to ask, "Do you love me?" and the husband certainly should not respond, "Oh, you know I do." That isn't enough. We must show it and say it: "I love you."

4. *Never be too proud to admit error and apologize.* Recently a woman expressed that in the twenty-five years she has been married, her husband has never said, "I'm sorry." I wonder if he has ever been able to admit to himself that he is wrong. Although his wife loves him dearly, she longs for the closeness the phrase "I'm sorry" could bring them.

37

One speaker suggested that the four most important words in the English language are "You may be right." The three most important are "I don't know." The two most important are "I'm sorry." The single most important word is "Thanks." The sentences are short and the words quite simple, but what magic they possess in communication!

A wise woman, Abigail, saved many lives by being big enough to apologize for the rudeness of her husband (I Samuel 25). Her husband died shortly thereafter, but Abigail went on to a happy and rewarding life. David, who later became king, was so impressed with her that he asked her to be his wife.

When a person receives an apology, he or she should do so graciously and not with an I-told-you-so attitude. The poet Ogden Nash aptly explained:

> To keep your marriage brimming
> With love in the loving cup,
> When you're wrong admit it,
> When you're right shut up.[4]

5. *Learn to accept suggestions.* A husband is not weak or inferior if he asks for the advice or opinion of his wife. The wife should consider it a compliment. The Bible records examples of women offering excellent advice to their husbands. In Judges 13, a wife offered encouraging wisdom to her frightened and perplexed husband who had experienced the visitation of an angel. Manoah exclaimed, "We shall surely die, because we have seen God." But his wife reassured him, "If the LORD were pleased to kill us he would not have received a burnt offering and a meat offering at our hands, neither would he have shewed us all these things, nor would as at this

time have told us such things as these" (Judges 13:22-23). (See also II Kings 4:8-10; Daniel 5:10-12; Matthew 27:19.)

The manner in which suggestions are made is also important. When spoken properly, ideas can fall like the welcomed gentle summer rain, but if barked, they may cause the spouse to run for cover.

6. *Do not use threats as leverage in communication.* For example, "If you continue fishing so much, I am going to start a hobby and make you stay home and take care of the kids." The complaint embodied in this threat may be legitimate, for spouses can be guilty of too much involvement in activities away from home. Lack of moderation in outside activities leaves the other partner feeling slighted or taken for granted. But threats are not the solution to this problem. Both husband and wife should sit down together and work out a compromise that is mutually agreeable.

7. *Plan both for family time and individual time.* Using the example just given, each spouse should allow the other time for pleasure and relaxation, but they should carefully consider the amount of time these outside hobbies take away from family time. Some activities may need to be eliminated or at least restricted to allow proper time for the family. Family-oriented activities would be good replacements.

Men need time for male companionship, participating in such activities as hunting, fishing, and sports. A wise wife considers the advantages of such activities for her husband both physically and emotionally. Likewise, men should understand that women also need a shopping trip with the girls or time just to be alone, away from the kids.

"You have the night off. Go shopping. I'll watch the kids" is a welcome surprise for any wife. The rejuvenating benefits to the wife are well worth the challenge of babysitting or the dollars spent.

Each partner should accept and try to understand the feelings of the other. Sensitivity is the key. One spouse should not base thoughts and actions on how he or she thinks the other person should feel. Both need to cultivate understanding and sensitivity.

8. *Good communication does not mean a passive attitude.* If the husband continually comes home to an unkempt house, no supper, and no note explaining when his wife will be home, he should not be expected merely to casually hint his disappointment. Neither should the wife have to sit around waiting for the husband, having no idea when he will arrive. There are certain basic responsibilities that a husband and wife can expect of each other. A matter-of-fact conversation can express feelings of disapproval and seek a remedy. The Scripture expresses, "How forcible are right words!" (Job 6:25).

9. *If in the course of a conversation you cannot reach general agreement, table the discussion until another time.* Angry verbal attacks should be avoided. For example, "You're just stubborn like your father" is a needless and loaded statement. The conversation must be kept on target. Words should not become barbed arrows of hate shot at each other. No one wins an argument. "There is only winning an agreement," says Denis Waitley.[5] If over a period of time a mutual compromise or agreement cannot be reached, and the situation adversely affects a marriage, the couple should seek proper, nonbiased counsel from a pastor or a professional counselor.

10. *The silent treatment, referred to as psychological divorce, can be devastating to any marriage.* The silent party may get his or her way but will often reap a harvest of frustration, anger, revenge, and infidelity in a mate. The silent treatment is the tactic of an immature adult. When we observe it in a child we call it pouting, but adults sometimes excuse their silence as pondering.

We were born with the need for communication. My wife heard about a man in his early twenties who was sentenced to five years in prison. Since he had been baptized in our church as an adolescent, she felt he was a prodigal son. She began to write to him and encourage him to recommit his life to the Lord. Surprisingly, the young man answered each of her letters and commented about each thought she shared with him. Nine months passed, and she continued writing, sometimes wondering how he really felt about her letters. One evening she was surprised to see a letter the young man had written in the local newspaper's column entitled "People's Sayso." Here is part of that letter:

> A preacher's wife writes me at least once a week, and I've never met this lady in my life. But still she writes and gives me some hope about getting out. If it wasn't for this lady writing me, I wouldn't get any mail at all.[6]

The remainder of his published letter did not reveal bitterness because his freedom was taken away. The author did not complain of inhumane jail conditions or tasteless food. There was no mention of his misfortunes in prison, although he was stabbed twelve times shortly after arrival.

Why had he written? He wanted to communicate. His friends were not writing, and he felt cut off and forgotten.

Communication is vital for the survival of any institution, especially the home. We sometimes wonder if we are getting through to our teenagers. Feedback is often limited. Positive results for our efforts may be slow in coming, but we must keep trying. To clam up, especially as a punishment to those we love, is harmful and inexcusable.

11. *Submissive whining is an unfair and childish communicative technique.* The aim of the whiner is to place the other person on a guilt trip. This brings some sense of personal victory to the whiner. The husband may say, "I'll cut back on my fishing because I love you, but I want you to know that I really enjoyed the relaxation it gave me." In other words, "Pat me on the back. I'm doing this for you, but don't you feel bad about forcing me to submit?"

12. *Laugh at yourself.* Things often happen in the home to cause the rest of the family to laugh at the unfortunate member. At one time or another each of us has been the one laughing or the one being laughed at. While painting a bedroom recently I stepped in my paint pan. I had two choices. I could either fuss, storm, kick the dog, and consider my family unappreciative, or laugh with them at me. Actually, laughter itself can be a form of communication. It can say, "Dad, we like you. You are human just like us kids. You make life fun." We should accept laughter and enjoy the opportunity to laugh together. "A merry heart doeth good like a medicine; but a broken spirit drieth the bones" (Proverbs 17:22).

13. *Base all communication decisions on God's Word.*

The Bible places certain responsibilities and roles on husband, wife, and children. Later chapters will discuss them at length.

14. *Pray together as a family.* A very important form of communication, family prayer is a sharing of needs, troubles, and thanksgiving with the Lord. Family prayer teaches and trains our children: "Mom and Dad have problems too, and they share those problems with God. God is their Father. Just as I have problems that I share with my earthly parents, so I should also discuss problems with my heavenly Father." By praying together we teach our children to communicate with the God who loves them even more than we do. What greater gift could we ever give our children? The old cliche, "The family that prays together, stays together," isn't outdated. I'm not suggesting prayers so lengthy that they become a drudgery for youngsters, but rather daily prayer together as a family.

15. *Eat meals together.* Mealtime should be a pleasant time of family togetherness, not the time to scold or correct. Emotional distress adversely affects digestion. Mealtime should be peaceful, with no negative conversation or griping allowed. The children should remain at the table for a determined period of time; they should not gobble down dinner in order to run out to play. Not only is this practice unhealthy and indicative of poor manners, but it prevents family communication. With patience and practice, mealtime can be a highlight of the day.

16. *Play with the children on their level.* Doing so takes expertise in role shifting. Shifting from plant manager or accounts receivable supervisor to parent and friend is difficult but essential. As the child grows older,

playing can include working on a project together, such as building a birdhouse or baking Christmas cookies. Vacations offer a wonderful opportunity for family play time.

A knot of fear gripped my stomach as I faced the roller coaster, but there beside me were two sons saying, "Ride it with us, Mom and Dad, please." We all got off feeling lightheaded but laughing. We did it together. The boys did not have to tell us how it felt. We shared the experience. The experience communicated an unspoken but real message: "We are a family, and we like being together."

Whether playing a game of checkers or racing around the block, the object is not to prove to self or the children that we are still the smartest or the strongest. The purpose of playing and competition is the growth of the children, mentally and physically. Properly handled, it is extremely enjoyable and rewarding.

A good test of parent-child rapport is whether or not the child shares with the parent his or her problems, questions, joys, and frustrations.

17. *Worship together.* The church is an extension of the home. It should not create division but should bring us to Christ as a family. Though a certain amount of segregation is profitable, the family sometimes needs to sit together in church rather than each always going separate ways. One religious professor suggested that the longevity of the Jewish faith can be attributed to their weekly (Sabbath) family worship, not only in the synagogue but also in the home.

18. *Establish a family night.* Clubs, school functions, and even church activities have often unintentionally robbed the home of its functions. Every home needs a

family night weekly, free of outside intrusion. The family should do something enjoyable together. This occasion is a wonderful opportunity for communication and growth.

19. *Forgive and forget.* Do not carry a grudge. As Christ has forgiven us, we are to forgive others completely (Ephesians 4:32). "And forgive us our debts, as we forgive our debtors" (Matthew 6:12).

20. *Be an initiator in the communication process.* Denis Waitley advises:

Take full responsibility for success in the communication process. As a listener, take full responsibility for hearing what the others are trying to say. As a talker, take full responsibility for being certain they understand what you are saying. Never meet anyone halfway in your relationships. Always give 100%.[7]

The father of a fifteen-year-old high school student who committed suicide filed suit against the school system. He claimed that the school was negligent in not recognizing the youth's signals that he was planning to take his life.[8] The court will have to make a decision on whether the school was at fault. Another question arises, however. Why did not the parents recognize the depression of their son? Parents should take personal responsibility for initiating communication. Blame shifting is a copout.

21. *Learn to live with the imperfect.* We dare not spend all our time trying to patch up all the little cracks in another's life. As George Eliot expressed:

Oh, the comfort, the inexpressible comfort, of feeling safe with a person, having neither to weigh thoughts nor measure words, but to pour them all out just as they are, chaff and grain together, knowing that a faithful hand will take and sift them, keep what is worth keeping, and then, with a breath of kindness, blow the rest away.[9]

Communication begins and continues with interest in someone. One of the major causes of communication difficulties in the home is lack of interest of the marriage partners in each other. After the wedding vows, each may take much for granted, often overlooking little things that count. The following communication test may reveal a lack of interest that affects communication.

1. When is your spouse's birthday?
2. What is your spouse's favorite color?
3. What is your spouse's favorite hobby?
4. When is your wedding anniversary?
5. How long have you been married?
6. What is your marriage partner's favorite restaurant?
7. What does your spouse want for Christmas?
8. What is your marriage partner's favorite song?
9. What is your spouse's favorite verse of Scripture?
10. What book is your spouse presently reading or has just finished?

Correct Answers _____

```
 9 – 10 correct answers . . . . . . . . . . . Excellent
 7 – 8   correct answers . . . . . . . . . . . Good
 5 – 6   correct answers . . . . . . . . . . . Fair
 3 – 4   correct answers . . . . . . . . . . . Unsatisfactory
 0 – 2   correct answers . . . . . . . . . . . You are not
                                               communicat-
                                               ing.
```

Time set aside daily to talk honestly, listen, and try to understand your spouse and children is very important. "The vacuum created by a failure to communicate will quickly be filled with rumor, misrepresentation, drivel and poison."[10] Recognizing that a communication gap exists is the beginning of improvement. Healing can then begin. But preaching sermons on communication is a backward step. A more positive approach would be taking a walk with a spouse or child, or initiating a conversation and listening interestedly. It may take time for the others to join in. Overnight success should not be expected after months or years of neglect. Good communication skills are not inherited; they are developed through practice.

The Foundation

"Just add a little dirt. It'll be okay." These were the pastor's instructions. The laborers were fellow parishioners; the project was a new educational facility. The project was to pour a foundation for a retaining wall. Work was progressing slowly, the cement truck arrived early, and the footer was not ready for pouring. The truck operator stood impatiently waiting. That's when the pastor suggested, "Just add a little dirt. It'll be okay."

A few days later the masons built a wall on the foundation. It took a few weeks for it to happen, but the wall began to tilt, first gradually, and then, tragically. The foundation was insufficient for building.

This story resembles a parable Jesus once told about two builders. One man, Jesus said, "built an house, and digged deep, and laid the foundation on a rock: and when the flood arose, the stream beat vehemently upon that house, and could not shake it: for it was founded upon a rock." The other, giving very little concern to the foundation and probably wanting to save time and effort, or else unknowledgeable of proper building procedures, "built an house upon the earth; against which the stream did beat vehemently, and immediately it fell; and the ruin of that house was great." (See Luke 6:48-49.)

In both accounts, the attention focuses not on the visible structure of the house but on the unseen part of the house, the foundation. Apart from the fact that Jesus was divine, possessing the characteristic of omniscience, He was likewise very knowledgeable on this subject from a human standpoint. Jesus was the son of a carpenter, and it is likely that He helped build a few of the houses in His hometown, Nazareth, before He began His ministry. He readily understood that the foundation is of utmost concern to any wise builder.

Two aspects of the foundation need consideration. First, the builder must consider nature. He must pour the foundation on solid ground and below the winter freeze line. This prevents sinking and shifting, cracking and crumbling as the ground freezes and thaws or is subjected to natural catastrophies such as an earthquake. To find a solid base, the builder must sometimes dig twenty, thirty, or more feet into the earth's surface. Second, the builder must have the right ingredients to make up the foundation. Today a proper concrete mixture of sand, gravel, and cement is poured into a web of reinforcement rods to form a solid base.

The foundation of a home likewise consists of two aspects. If either is missing or lacking, a home is vulnerable. Let's look at these two aspects of a home's foundation: the base offered by Christ, and the ingredients poured in by the husband and the wife.

The Base Christ Offers

A songwriter beautifully expressed our sure foundation in Christ:

> On Christ the solid rock I stand;
> All other ground is sinking sand,
> All other ground is sinking sand.[1]

No home is secure that is not built upon faith in Christ and His Word. For this reason, Scripture instructs, "Be ye not unequally yoked together with unbelievers: for what fellowship hath righteousness with unrighteousness? and what communion hath light with darkness?" (II Corinthians 6:14). A Christian should not marry a non-Christian. To disobey this command is sin.

Such a union is like yoking together a donkey and an ox. This union of animals has numerous problems: different heights, different speeds, different strides. The two are not compatible. They make a poor team. They pull against each other instead of with each other. A marriage of a Christian and a non-Christian is comparably unequal. The two have different needs, goals, and futures. Eternity brings separation. The children are pulled between the love for two parents, each going in separate directions.

This admonition is not meant to frustrate those who are already married to non-Christians, but it is intended to reinforce the biblical command for the unmarried believer to marry "only in the Lord" (I Corinthians 7:39). The next chapter provides suggestions and encouragement for those Christians who are already married to non-Christians.

There are numerous advantages to a home built upon the foundation of Christ.

1. *Each partner shares common interests.* They go

to church together. Many shared activities will be family and church related. Interest in music is similar—different styles perhaps, but religious. Many of their friends will be in church, and they too share similar interests. Because of these common interests, each will be uplifted—drawn nearer to the Lord and one another.

2. *Each shares common goals.* They will both strive to please Christ. Whether in educational pursuits, occupation, or recreation, a Christian home has Christ as the center of life's goals. And, of course, each person shares the ultimate hope of eternal life with Christ.

3. *Each shares the same moral disciplines.* The family is not divided by love for the world. Entertainment is Christian in nature. The home is not plagued by alcohol or drug use. The children are instructed both at home and in church on how to behave themselves while dating. Premarital sex is known to be morally wrong. Husband and wife share the same belief in fidelity.

4. *The children are raised according to scriptural disciplines.* Neither parent follows secular philosophies of liberalism.

5. *The marriage is based upon scriptural guidelines.* The Bible explains the roles of both husband and wife. One prominent passage on this subject is Ephesians 5:22-33:

Wives, submit yourselves unto your own husbands, as unto the Lord. For the husband is the head of the wife, even as Christ is the head of the church: and he is the saviour of the body. Therefore, as the church is subject unto Christ, so let the wives be to their own husbands in every thing. Husbands, love your wives, even as Christ also loved the church, and gave himself for it; that he might sanctify and cleanse it with the washing of water by the word, that he might present it to himself a glorious church, not having spot, or wrinkle, or any such thing; but that it should be holy and without blemish. So ought men to love their wives as their own bodies. He that loveth his wife loveth himself. For no man ever yet hated his own flesh; but nourisheth and cherisheth it, even as the Lord the church; for we are members of his body, of his flesh, and of his bones. For this cause shall a man leave his father and mother, and shall be joined unto his wife, and they two shall be one flesh. This is a great mystery; but I speak concerning Christ and the church. Nevertheless let every one of you in particular so love his wife even as himself; and the wife see that she reverence her husband.

According to this passage the wife is to submit—to yield to the authority of her husband. Our submission to Christ is voluntary; Christ does not make us submit. We do it out of love, respect, and appreciation for Calvary. We do not consider it a drudgery, but an honor. The wife should exemplify this same type of submission to her husband. Christ's order of authority calls for the husband to lead the home. He should not have to struggle for this leadership; the wife should voluntarily submit.

This submission does not depict a king-servant relationship, but rather a partnership in which both are of equal worth and value and in which the husband assumes the primary leadership responsibility. Any idea that the husband can dictate to his wife, abuse her, or make arbitrary decisions regarding her is excluded when we look at the husband's role.

The key word in this passage for the husband's duty may surprise some. It is not "provider" nor "disciplinarian," although these roles are part of his duty. Instead, this passage stresses love, stating three times for the husband to love his wife (Ephesians 5:25, 28, 33). Once it tells the husband to love as Christ loves the church. Twice it tells him to love her as he loves himself.

This kind of love blends or joins the man and woman together. Too often a husband wants his wife to be the primary one to manifest love. He prefers to sit back and soak in all the compliments, sweet talk, and attention. But the Bible places the responsibility to promote love primarily on the husband. He is to be the initiator of love within the home.

The husband is to love his wife "even as Christ also loved the church" (Ephesians 5:25). How did Christ love the church? He displayed sacrificial love. He gave His life for the church. (Husband, do you love your wife that much? Would you die, if necessary, for her? Or will you die if in order to please her you are not able to go fishing as often as you would like?) A wife is more meaningful than life. A husband should be willing to give up any earthly thing for her.

Jacob was very much in love with Rachel, and surely Rachel loved Jacob. "And Jacob served seven years for Rachel; and they seemed unto him but a few days, for the love he had to her" (Genesis 29:20). Today, some would say, "Jacob, you're hen-pecked." Not so! The Bible calls his attitude love—genuine, conjugal, husband-wife love. We would see a noticeable drop in the divorce rates if more men followed this example of love today. Too many men would rather fight for their right to go fishing instead of mowing the lawn for their wives. Some would even go fishing and leave the wife mowing.

The two marriage partners are no longer two separate entities, but they become "one flesh" (Genesis 2:24). A husband harms himself when he refuses to love his wife properly. "So ought men to love their wives as their own bodies. He that loveth his wife loveth himself" (Ephesians 5:28). If a man loves his wife, he is putting a feather in his own cap. He has no right to treat her harshly or dictatorially. "Husbands, love your wives, and be not bitter against them" (Colossians 3:19).

The apostle Peter also gave instructions to both husband and wife that were inspired of God (I Peter 3:1-7). Like Paul, Peter taught that wives should submit to their husbands. He described this act of submission as an inward beauty that far exceeds any external adornment. In fact, verse 1 explains that a wife's submissive spirit can cause an unbelieving husband to find Christ. In turn, verse 7 exhorts the husband to be understanding of the wife and to give her honor.

The woman is different from the man. Physically, she is weaker in most cases, and the husband should not expect his wife to equal his physical abilities. Forty hours at the factory, raising three children, and taking care of a husband, house, two cats, and a dog may be too much for her. Unless the husband understands this, he may come home to a "Dear John" letter. The wife is different mentally, not in intellectual ability but in the way she thinks. Her hormones, genes, and temperament are all different. Her emotions can be affected by hormonal changes, and her husband should be aware of these changes. He should seek to understand her, not merely to stay out of her hair when she does not act in a manner that he considers "normal." The Lord uses some leverage to get the husband to love his wife and to give her honor: "That your prayers be not hindered" (I Peter 3:7). A lack of love can result in unanswered prayers.

A husband's love causes him to submit to his wife's wishes and desires as much as to his own (Ephesians 5:21, 28), and it gives his wife the confidence to submit to his family leadership. A wife's submission includes love for her husband (Titus 2:4). Thus a biblical marriage is a partnership in which the husband and wife are "heirs together of the grace of life" (I Peter 3:7) and which is characterized by mutual submission, respect, and love. Their roles are different but complementary and of equal importance in the family, church, and society.

Many marriages fail because people fail to abide by these simple scriptural guidelines. Some people think, I'll follow these principles if my spouse will, but the biblical commands are unconditional. One spouse's disobedience should not affect the other spouse's willingness to obey the Scriptures.

6. *The Christian family can experience agape love, divine love.* While the world is hating and murdering its own, we can be blessed with the love offered by Jesus Christ. This self-sacrificial love can be a part of our Christian home. The characteristics of such love are beautiful:

Unchangeable. "Jesus . . . having loved his own which were in the world, he loved them unto the end" (John 13:1).

Self-sacrificing. "Greater love hath no man than this, that a man lay down his life for his friends" (John 15:13).

Inseparable. "Who shall separate us from the love of

56

Christ? shall tribulation, or distress, or persecution, or famine, or nakedness, or peril, or sword?" (Romans 8:35).

Lasting. "I have loved thee with an everlasting love" (Jeremiah 31:3).

Unconditional. "But God commendeth his love toward us, in that, while we were yet sinners, Christ died for us" (Romans 5:8).

Unmerited. "Behold, what manner of love the Father hath bestowed upon us, that we should be called the sons of God" (I John 3:1).

Recently, a young boy, in a rage of anger, fatally shot his mother and seriously wounded his father and younger brother. All of this was the result of a family argument. How tragic! But consider the protection offered by a Christian home. We are not naturally immune to certain diseases, but a vaccination can greatly reduce our chances of contracting disease. Such is the case in a Christian home. The love of Christ offers us a spiritual vaccination. It greatly reduces our susceptibility to destructive diseases that can attack our home.

The Poured Foundation

The second aspect of the foundation of our home is what we put into our marriage and family. Both husband and wife must share equally in this responsibility. Each must put into the marriage a vow of commitment—"till death do us part"—"an unconditional commitment to an imperfect person."[2]

Often, a major weakness in the foundation of a marriage is the lack of commitment. A young couple asked a minister to perform their wedding ceremony. The prospective bride, already the victim of one failed marriage, shocked him with her request, "Could you omit 'till death do us part'?" She was not working on the foundation, but on an escape plan—just in case marriage number two did not work out.

The Western concept of marriage has evolved into almost everything except commitment. The marriage vow is pleasant traditional-religious rhetoric, but often it is not realistically believed. Books and movies paint a picture of marriage as an emotional bliss that is attained in a few hours. They focus mostly on the romantic relationship. These distorted views are often buttressed by at least one extramarital or premarital affair. As another example, Robin Adams Sloan's "Gossip Column" covers the many failures and new attempts of marriage between celebrities. But we dare not copy Hollywood's facade of happiness and abandon biblical marriage.

In biblical and even colonial times parents typically planned the marriages of their children. Sometimes the engaged couple did not meet before the wedding or else saw each other briefly in the presence of parents. But divorce in those times was almost unheard of. Ernest W. Burgess writes, "The change from marriages arranged by parents to those entered into by young people on their own initiative has not increased the stability of marriage. Judging by the increase in the divorce rate, free choice seems to have had the reverse effect."

While I am glad that I had the privilege of selecting my wife, the reason that marriages arranged by parents outlived many of today's marriages is that modern society has an inadequate concept of love. Something is amiss: a lack of commitment. Like a superglue on today's market that bonds only when two mixtures are combined, a marriage without commitment makes for a sticky mess, but no stability. Marriages of the past usually lasted because they were founded upon commitment, even when there was little romance at first, but many modern marriages fail because they are founded only upon romance and not commitment.

Commitment is not mere emotionalism. Emotions change with circumstances—and especially time. Scientists suggest that our moods can change in accordance with the color someone wears. Emotions are at their best fickle.

It is no wonder that so many are leaving their marriage spouses. Like chasing after an elusive dream, some seek that "perfect" mate. Commitment says, "No matter what life serves us, we'll eat it together." Someone explained commitment by surveying a meal of bacon and eggs. The chicken was dedicated, but the pig was committed.

Time did not stand still for a certain man's once-beautiful bride, nor was she immune to the raging disease that left her an invalid. And yet, every Sunday, there they were together in church. He wheeled her to the vestibule and hesitated while someone checked the ladies' room. Once clear, he gently lifted her limp body from the chair and carried her in. He was commitment personified!

If both are committed to Christ and committed to each other, a couple has a foundation upon which to build a beautiful home. This foundation does not exempt them from life's tragedies. They will come. The winds will blow, the rain will beat upon the house, and the earth around may quake violently, but the home need not crumble. Damaged? Maybe. Destroyed? No.

On a trip my wife and I took, the huge plane banked gently as it descended through the clouds hovering over Mexico City. Below loomed the Sunday afternoon attraction, the arena for bull fighting. Gigantic snow-capped mountains—Sierra Nevada, Popocatepeth, and Ixtacihuath—towered in the distance. Nancy and I stepped off the plane, thrilled by the anticipation of a week's vacation in Mexico. It seemed strange to have landed and still be one and one-half miles above sea level.

Founded in A.D. 1300, Mexico City spreads for miles over an oval-shaped basin that at one time was nearly covered by the combined water of three lakes—Chalco, Xochimilco, and Texcoco. A project to drain the lakes began in colonial times but was not completed until the twentieth century. A spongy, unstable layer of subsoil was left. This layer provided a poor foundation for building. Proof of this is evident in the many structures we visited. Some of them had sunk as much as an entire floor into the ground. Cracks had developed in many of the buildings. Others tilted as if tired from standing so many years. Though centuries old, they were still standing. Their longevity was a result of colossal foundations. Through years of frequent, minor tremors, and occasionally violent earthquakes, these buildings had survived. They were "built upon a rock."

Shortly following our return from Mexico, we were shocked to hear of the earthquake that devastated parts of Mexico City. It was not surprising to hear, however, that many of the historic attractions we had visited were still standing—damaged, but standing. The greatest destruction came to more modern buildings, buildings that visiting engineers speculated were built with inadequate foundations, insufficient depth, and improper concrete mixtures of cement, sand, and gravel. What a tragedy! Thousands were injured and left homeless, and many died. Perhaps the consequences of this quake would have been less severe with proper building foundations.

With the North American divorce rate worse than at any time in our history, it is time to shore up the foundation of our homes. The foundation mentioned in the beginning of this chapter never did fall. It would have, had we not worked diligently in securing it. It required a lot of extra work, but we were able to save it. Nor is it too late for our homes. Jesus Christ can help us strengthen our foundation. He can be the chief cornerstone. Likewise, we can incorporate into our home a fresh commitment that can solidify our family structure. Extra work? Yes, but we must do it. Let us dig deep and build upon Christ. Let us pour ourselves into our marriages. And let us start today!

Framing Up the House

*W*hen considering the framework of a house, one word is paramount: support. The framework is a support network throughout the house. The roof cannot be constructed until supporting walls are in place. Doors, windows, electrical outlets, and ceiling all depend on the framework.

As a house must have a support system of walls, both husband and wife fulfill certain roles that support the marriage. They can build a lasting and lovely home on this support.

The dictionary offers varied meanings for this seemingly simple word. To support means

1. Keep from falling; hold up
2. Give strength or courage to
3. Provide for
4. Maintain, keep up, or keep going
5. Be in favor of; back
6. Help prove; bear out

    7. Endure, especially with patience or
       fortitude
    8. Assist or protect[1]

These definitions describe the supportive roles of a husband and wife.

The Husband's Supportive Role
in the Home

The husband's first and most important role is to be a Christian. This role does not mean participating in a building program, or serving on the deacon board, or attending most church services, although these aspects are important. This role refers to a genuine commitment to Jesus Christ—at church, yes, but especially in the privacy of the home. The husband needs to demonstrate this commitment in his home by his spiritual leadership. He should implement personal devotions, prayer, and Bible reading, and provide spiritual guidance to the family by word and example. The home preceded the church, the patriarch preceded the preacher. It is possible to have a spiritual home without having a revival church, but not a revival church without spiritual homes. One author called the home "the suburb of heaven."[2] Some churches, laden with problems, are the result of spiritual neglect in the home.

Every family needs the husband/father to lead it. The wife and children seldom verbally request, "Dad, be our leader." But they need his leadership, and deep down they yearn for it. Charlie W. Shedd explains this concept in his book *Letters to Philip*, but he offers some cautions as well:

There are dozens of ways you might hear this: "Get control!" "Seize command!" "Run the show!" "Grab the reins!" "Call the signals!" "Stay at the helm!" "Steer your ship!" "Name the tunes!" "Bring 'em to heel!" "Sit on the lid!" Any variation will do provided you learn that there is a delicate line between "just enough" and "too much."

The image here is not that of a mighty potentate sitting on his throne, ruling his cowering subjects with an iron hand. This is more like a conductor standing on his box directing a symphony. Delicate, but definite! Subdued, yet powerful![3]

A reminiscing adult stated, "One of my most memorable and cherished moments with my father was a time when he exerted his leadership in my life. Dad, though a man of few words, managed to give this love-struck teenager a lecture on dating. It was instructive, yet reprimanding. He encouraged and cautioned. I could tell he didn't particularly enjoy the task. I loved it. It said to me, 'Dad knows, he cares, and I am not alone.' "

Some husbands/fathers delegate too much of their spiritual responsibility. They expect the church alone to teach their family Bible doctrine. They assume the Sunday school teacher has taught little Johnny basic Bible stories. Surely the youth leader has instructed their teenager in Christian dating principles, they think.

In a classic example, a husband expressed disappointment in his church because he thought it had neglected to teach his wife. He complained that she no longer wanted to attend the church and their children were following her example. Was the church at fault, or was it his lack of leadership? Either is tragic. Both are responsible. But let us notice the biblical command for home leadership: "And thou shalt teach them [Bible truths] diligently unto thy children, and shalt talk of them when thou sittest in thine house, and when thou walkest by the way, and when thou liest down, and when thou risest up. . . . And thou shalt write them upon the posts of thy house, and on thy gates" (Deuteronomy 6:7, 9). What place of instruction does this passage emphasize? The home!

A father/husband teaches by two means: verbal instruction and instruction by example. Examples sometimes nullify verbal instructions. Once, a couple became engaged in a heated argument just prior to going to church. They hurled hateful words at each other. While the wife sat sulking throughout the evening service, her husband slowly rose during testimony service to share his love and appreciation for Christ. With his wife pulling on his coattail accusingly, he glanced down at her and exclaimed, "It's you I'm mad at, not God!"

The following poem expresses so well the need to set a good example in Christianity.

Walk a Little Plainer, Daddy

Walk a little plainer, Daddy,
Said a little boy so frail.
I'm following in your footsteps
And I don't want to fail.
Sometimes your steps are very plain,
Sometimes they are hard to see.
So walk a little plainer, Dad,
For you are leading me.

I know that once you walked this way
Many years ago,
And what you did along the way
I'd really like to know;
For sometimes when I am tempted
I don't know what to do.
So walk a little plainer, Daddy,
For I must follow you.

Someday when I'm grown up—
You are like I want to be.
Then I will have a little boy
Who will want to follow me;
And I would want to lead him right
And help him to be true.
So walk a little plainer, Daddy,
For we must follow you.

      —Author unknown

  The life of Ahab, ungodly king of Israel, exemplifies this principle in a negative fashion. He trained his son by his example to do evil. It is no small wonder that his son, Ahaziah, "did evil in the sight of the LORD, and walked in the way of his father" (I Kings 22:52).

  The second role for the husband is to be *a husband*. This sounds like a superfluous statement, but it expresses an important truth. The only way to tell that some men are married to their wives is that they have the same last name and address. Otherwise, the pair seems to be incompatible, uncaring strangers. This situation does not have to be. With effort and consideration a man can become the husband his wife truly adores. To be a good husband a man must remember these four points: a wife is different from her husband, yet she is equal to him; she is complementary to him, but not in competition with him.

Women have proven their worth as doctors, lawyers, astronauts, and business executives. A retired Air Force colonel recently stated, "Women would make better navigators than most men because of their attention to detail." The wise husband understands and appreciates his wife's abilities. A woman's physical makeup is different but not inferior. Emotionally women are different, too. For example, crying is typically a normal emotional outlet for her that does not need a reason according to masculine thinking.

Too many men exemplify the comic character Hagar the Horrible by being insensitive to their wife's work. For example, both husband and wife may work on a secular job. Arriving home after eight hours on the job, he retires to his easy chair to read the paper while she goes to the kitchen and prepares dinner. After dinner, she does the dishes while he retreats to his woodshop to make finishing touches on a hobby. While she finishes the laundry he soaks in the tub. The unspoken philosophy here is "My job is in the factory; at home my time is my own." True, but what about the wife?

The wife deserves equal treatment. Sharing chores is truly caring. The father should share the responsibility of raising the children. Changing diapers and night duty are not for mothers only. A father who refuses to help in those areas is robbing himself of a deeper relationship with his children.

A wife is a complement, not a competitor. Often she excels in certain areas. Her achievements do not discredit male ability or suggest competition. If the wife wins at Scrabble, wonderful! Her ability with words may be beneficial with her husband's next job report. Likewise, the husband can help the wife with his abilities in certain areas. Dorothy praised her husband, "I am so thankful for Ed. He always sees to oil changes and keeps the car in perfect working order. All I have to do is turn the key." And so it is—the man and woman bring separate, different abilities and become one, making those separate abilities a blessing to each other.

Here are some suggestions to help a couple get on the road to married bliss.

- Keep romance in the marriage.
- Court to stay out of court.
- Plan one date a week without the children or business associates.
- Take many mini vacations.
- Husbands, always treat your wife like a lady. Work as hard to keep her as you did to get her. Open doors for her, say "thank you," and compliment her often (sincerely). Be thoughtful enough to carry heavy objects for her, including the babies and groceries.
- Never, never forget special dates such as birthday and anniversary. To remember means to act upon the occasion. Husbands, when birthdays bring your wife the blues, like at age forty, be understanding and do something extra special for her, including forgetting her age.

Charles Shedd offers six nevers for the husband:

1. Never point in derision to something she can't change.
2. Never criticize her in public.
3. Never compare her unfavorably with other women. (This includes your mother.)
4. Never drop a delayed bomb. Example: Suddenly telling her you don't like something she's been doing a long time.
5. Never go away when she is crying.
6. Never lay a hand on her except in love.[4]

Daily practice of the above principles is a key to success.

A husband is responsible for fulfilling the physical and emotional needs of his wife. Problems develop when a husband views sex as a personally gratifying experience only, overlooking the equally important needs of his wife in this area. A marriage will be much smoother when the husband realizes his wife has similar needs. A marriage partner may have hangups about the sexual relationship, sometimes viewing it as bothersome, frustrating, distasteful, or even unspiritual. But it is important to recognize that this part of marriage is ordained by God.

The Bible instructs both husbands and wives to fulfill each other's sexual needs: "Let the husband render unto the wife due benevolence: and likewise also the wife unto the husband. The wife hath not power of her own body, but the husband: and likewise also the husband hath not power of his own body, but the wife. Defraud ye not one the other, except it be with consent for a time, that ye may give yourselves to fasting and prayer; and come together again, that Satan tempt you not for your incontinency" (I Corinthians 7:3-5).

A husband who dutifully tries to schedule love some-where in his busy routine, with a time limit attached, can be unromantic. Instead, he should be an affectionate lover who offers an unexpected morning embrace that sets the mood for romance later, and who does not rush through romantic times.

The total person is involved in the marriage rela-tionship—physically, emotionally, socially, and spiritual-ly. The union of a man and woman is complex. They are such opposites—like sandpaper and satin—yet the two become one. The "one flesh" is not simply the husband or the wife, but the sum of both, and an important aspect of this union is the sexual relationship.

Lovemaking involves sharing, learning, and growing together. Not everything comes naturally. No one is born a good husband or a good lover. Rather, the physical ex-pression of love is a learned response that can improve.

A husband must not expect his wife to comform total-ly to his predetermined ideas of lovemaking. *The Act of Marriage* by Tim and Beverly LaHaye is an excellent, thorough discussion of this subject from a Christian view-point, and it contains much helpful advice for overcom-ing problems. A person should not be too proud or too embarrassed to seek help in this area. If a problem exists that cannot be solved by the husband and wife together, they should seek the kind of help offered by the book, and if necessary, seek the counsel of a qualified Christian.

A person should never deny lovemaking in order to get even or use it as leverage to get one's way. Such childish and selfish tactics leave permanent scars.

Abigail Van Buren offers *Ten Commandments for the Husband:*

71

1. Thou shalt put thy wife before thy mother, thy father, thy daughter, and thy son, for she is thy lifelong companion.
2. Abuse not thy body either with excessive food, tobacco or drink, that thy days may be many and healthful in the presence of thy loved ones.
3. Permit neither thy business, nor thy hobby, to make of thee a stranger to thy children, for the precious gift a man giveth his family is his time.
4. Forget not the virtue of cleanliness.
5. Make not thy wife a beggar, but share willingly with her thy worldly goods.
6. Forget not to say, "I love you." For even though thy love be constant, thy wife doth yearn to hear the words.
7. Remember that the approval of thy wife is worth more than the admiring glances of a hundred strangers. Cleave unto her and forsake all others.
8. Keep thy home in good repair, for out of it cometh the joy of thy old age.
9. Forgive with grace, for who among us does not need to be forgiven?
10. Honor the Lord thy God all the days of thy life, and thy children will rise up and call thee blessed.[5]

Every wife has a right to ask these ten things of a Christian husband.

The husband should refrain from flattering words or flirtatious gestures toward other women. Though he may be morally innocent, a husband cannot control how another woman will interpret his actions or remarks. Would he want another man making the same gestures or comments to his wife? This question is a good guide to follow in dealing with other women, whether in the office, in a restaurant, or at a church picnic. Often, jealousy on the part of the wife is a natural response to the manner in which her husband conducts himself—from remarks to wandering eyes.

Other responsibilities of a husband are maintenance around the house, mowing the lawn, washing the car, and painting the fence. A wife should not have to beg her husband to fulfill these responsibilities. What he cannot or does not do, he should arrange for someone else to do. She may not always compliment him, but she will be appreciative of his efforts in these areas, and she will express that appreciation to her friends.

Finally the husband should take time and care to enjoy life, and not let it become a burdensome chore. "Live joyfully with the wife whom thou lovest" (Ecclesiastes 9:9). Life is not all work; it is fun too. The Lord wants men and women to enjoy marriage. Our attitude about marriage makes all the difference. A sweet fragrance exists in every husbandly chore when we slow down and enjoy the scenery. Rolf Turnbull stated, "Life is not for work, but work for life, and when it is carried to the extent of undermining life or unduly absorbing it, work is not praiseworthy but blameworthy."[6]

The husband's third supportive role is to be *a father*. Rearing children is a joint effort. A father's involvement is essential. A child has certain needs that only a father can fulfill properly. A son needs to learn from Dad how to throw a ball, cast a line, or change the oil in the lawn mower. Johnny's mother is wonderful, but he needs Dad to teach him how to be a man. Although a wife will teach her daughter to be a lady, the father's life plays a key role in helping develop his daughter's attitude towards men.

Proper parenting, though full of joys, does not come through haphazard or happenstance efforts. It is a task. A plaque says it well: "Anyone can be a father, but it takes a special person to be a dad." Because of the importance of this role, chapter 5 deals with parenting.

The fourth area of the husband's responsibility is to be *the provider* for the family. "But if any provide not for his own, and specially for those of his own house, he hath denied the faith, and is worse than an infidel" (I Timothy 5:8). Although money cannot buy happiness, statistics indicate that if a family has a comfortable income it has a greater chance of having a happy home. If a man is nothing more to his family than money, however, he is a poor husband and father. Since so much of life revolves around finance, chapter 7 is devoted to this subject.

The Wife's Supportive Role in the Home

Like the husband, a wife's most important role is to be *a Christian.* It is easy for a person to become so caught up in Christian service that she neglects devotion to Christ. She can become so busy working for God that she fails to walk with God. Church can be demanding: showers, weddings, ladies' group, Sunday school class, bake sales, sewing circle, outreach, nursery duty, choir practice, and so on. But a merry-go-round of never-ending service to the church offers little time for personal devotion to Christ.

The biblical account of Mary and Martha is a good

example. Martha was busy preparing and serving refreshments, refilling drinks, and washing dishes. She was really doing everything right for her special guest. All the while, Mary sat at the feet of Jesus, drinking in every word that flowed from a reservoir of spiritual knowledge. Finally, Martha could stand it no longer. To build a case to support her accusations of Mary's neglect of womanly duties, she asked Jesus for His unbiased opinion. He quickly but kindly replied, "Martha, Martha, thou art careful [worried] and troubled about many things: but one thing is needful: and Mary hath chosen that good part, which shall not be taken away from her" (Luke 10:41-42).

A wife should evaluate her Christian life with this account, asking herself, "Have I chosen that good part? Am I taking enough time to sit at the feet of Jesus?" Christianity encompasses both service to the needs of humanity and devotion to Christ. We must keep both aspects in balance.

The second support role is to be *a wife*. Motherhood is important, but the wife should not minimize the responsibility of being a wife. Some husbands are placed on the back burner while their wife spends all waking hours tending to the needs of the children. A wife who does this will eventually hurt herself. The children will grow up and leave home, and her responsibilities will decrease. She will then have time for her husband, but he will have adjusted through the years and learned to get along without a close relationship with his wife. The silence and loneliness of an empty house can overwhelm her. She can be crushed and will not understand why his love has grown cold. The back burner is not sufficient! One husband teasingly reminded his wife, "Just remember, I was here before

75

the children, and when they are gone I will be all you have left." In the middle years while the children are growing up, the wife should not neglect the needs of her husband.

Many wives, especially working women, are often expected to take care of all the home responsibilities. Some are overworked to the point of not having time for their husbands. The family can alleviate this problem by sharing the chores at home. The husband and children will be more apt to help if they are rewarded with more time with Mom.

The following is a suggested list of do's and don'ts for the wife. Though addressed to the wife, many of them apply to the husband as well.

Do's

1. Appreciate your husband. Thank him occasionally for supplying the family needs or cleaning the car or taking you shopping. Everyone needs to know he is appreciated. Work is much more enjoyable when it is appreciated. Do not assume he knows how much you appreciate him. Tell him.

2. If you must disagree, do so respectfully. Show him respect in public and in private. The wounds inflicted by putdowns, especially those in public, are difficult to heal. Even though you may apologize later, he will have lingering embarrassment every time he faces those who witnessed the situation.

3. Allow your husband to be the spiritual leader in the home. If he is reluctant to accept this responsibility, offer encouragement. A young man was too shy to offer thanks before a meal. Through the positive attitude of his wife, he is now able to give Bible lessons at church.

4. Tell him how important he is to you. Allow him to know that you feel safer when he is present.

5. Do things that especially please him or pleasantly surprise him. Occasionally, have a hot tub of water waiting for him when you know he has had a particularly hard day at work. Thoughtfulness on your part can make a husband long to go home in the evening instead of somewhere with the guys.

6. Recognize and compliment his positive attributes. The male ego is real and needs to be fed to stay healthy. He will not need the attention of others if he is well taken care of at home.

7. Unless there are serious reasons for doubt in a certain area, trust him. Stay away from romance novels that paint a picture of all males as unfaithful. A mind fed on good thoughts will not live in fear if the husband is five minutes late.

8. Keep the house tidy, but do not let this task consume all your time. Make your home a place that your husband is happy to bring his friends to.

9. Plan nourishing meals. High dosages of sweets and fats may delight his taste buds but destroy his health. Serve the meals attractively. Milk cartons, bread bags, and other such food storage paraphernalia should not clutter the table. Make your mealtime a special time of family togetherness.

10. Keep romance in the marriage. While you should not have to compete for his affection, he should never be tempted to look elsewhere for romance because he is denied it at home. Robert Taylor points out, "When the urge to stray enters, the gate has often been unlatched from inside the home. Bolt the door!"[7] Keep life exciting.

11. Be clean and dress attractively. Your appearance is a source of pleasure to your husband. Learn to fix your hair and take the time to do it. Do you remember how you made sure everything was just so for a date before you were married? Marriage does not change his desire for you to be well groomed and smelling sweet. And do not forget your smile. Years of togetherness must not rob you of the simple joys of life. Look forward to his arrival each evening. Do not take it for granted.

Don'ts

1. Don't compare him to other men unless it is in a positive sense.

2. Don't question his fidelity without having reasonable proof. Realize that everyone is subject to physical attractions but that does not mean your husband has yielded to temptation mentally or physically. Don't drive your husband into the arms of another by constant accusations.

3. Don't force your husband into situations that would promote infidelity. As an example, consider the wife who has her husband constantly running errands for her female friend who has recently gone through a divorce. Such a friend's problem may become yours.

4. Don't overburden your husband financially. When you are aware that a new bedroom suite will not fit into your budget, there is no need to mention your desire for it. To do so may cause him to go into needless debt—debt that puts a strain on your credit and brings turmoil into a home. You may have your new bedroom suite, but your husband may sleep on the couch. You can sleep better on box springs in peace and harmony than in bitterness on satin sheets and a Serta mattress.

5. Don't criticize him in front of your children. You will probably kiss and make up, but the children will have lasting memories of the negative remarks. If you must discuss an unpleasant subject, wait until the time is right. A better time is when he is well fed, not overly tired or under excessive pressure on the job, and in private.

6. Don't burden him with unreasonable chores around the house. Be understanding of the mental stress that accompanies his dog-eat-dog occupation, and allow him some time to unwind with a hobby or sport.

7. Don't expect your husband to come home from work feeling like a dynamo—especially after age thirty. He may not be in a romantic mood even if you're wearing your most attractive dress. It does not mean you are no longer desirable to him, but only that he has had a very taxing day. His adrenalin may have been spent on production, tight schedules, overbearing bosses, and rush-hour traffic. Of course, he may want physical affection when he arrives home. Be responsive to him in this area. Momentary thrills offered by other women are no match for the long-range dividends of having a wife who thoroughly enjoys her husband's romantic attention.

8. Don't approach him in a negative, demanding manner. For example, "The car is a filthy mess. I don't know why you haven't washed it!" He may retaliate defensively, obstinately, or insultingly. Why not try a more gentle approach: "You sure made the car look nice last week when you washed it. Do you think you will be able to find time to do it again this week?" Be able to accept a negative response.

9. Don't demand that he conform to your ways overnight. It may take some time for him to catch on to put-

ting his shoes in a certain place or hanging his clothes a certain way. Be patient. By reminding from time to time without anger or sarcasm, you can plant seeds that will bring forth much fruit in the future. If his mother allowed him to behave in such a manner for eighteen years plus, the habit will take some time to correct.

10. Don't allow yourself to become a servant to food. It is important that you do your best to remain healthy and physically attractive. If you have an excessive appetite, seek help. Consult a physician to help you lose excess pounds and maintain a proper weight. Being physically fit will help you have a good attitude and will aid your self-esteem. Both are helpful in being a happy wife.

11. Don't be in competition with your husband. Be a team player, not demanding personal praise for accomplishments. Even if he gets all the credit, it is still a compliment to you because he is your man.

The high cost of living makes many wives feel compelled to help with the family budget. Without giving much consideration to all her other responsibilities and contributions to her family, she may plunge headlong into the job market. Often she spends much of what she earns on a babysitter, a second car to get her to work, and appropriate clothing for her job. The wife/mother should thoroughly consider the advantages and disadvantages of leaving home for the office—especially before the children are of school age.

A recent study reveals that many successful businessmen are benefited more by a wife who works at home rather than the office. In an article entitled "Ordinary Millionaires," Beth Brophy and Gordon Witkin write, "A stable home life with few outside distractions provides the ordinary millionaire with stamina to persevere in business. Most of them have lasting marriages, often to their high school or college sweetheart, and millionaire wives are unlikely to work outside the home."[8] The men in this study were not born millionaires. They acquired their wealth by hard work and good business sense, while the wife took care of the home.

This is not to say that a wife cannot take care of the home adequately and work on an outside job, but an outside job for the wife is not always the answer to financial needs. It can sometimes create more difficult problems. And the wife who chooses to work in the home should not feel that she is depriving her family of financial prosperity. Moreover, there are some jobs the wife can do in the home to bring in extra income. Or she may help her husband's business by doing the bookkeeping, answering the business phone, typing letters, and so on at home. Chapter 8 discusses the woman who works outside the home.

The third support role of the wife is to be a good *mother*. The next chapter will deal more thoroughly with child rearing, but let us consider the influence the mother has upon her children. She spends far more time with the children than the husband does. The mother will tremendously affect the child's attitude about life, others, the father, and most importantly, the Lord. One son reported, "Though my dad became a Christian before I was born, none of us children followed his example. It was when Mom surrendered to Christ that we made a start for God. I was fifteen years old."

The Bible contains many examples of the influence of the mother. Ahaziah was forty-two years old when he was made king of Judah. He wore the crown only one year in Jerusalem. He accomplished nothing worthy of spiritual mention. Instead, he did evil. The Scripture gives us an accurate account of his reign in few and easily understood words: "He also walked in the ways of the house of Ahab: for his mother was his counseller to do wickedly" (II Chronicles 22:3).

We also see the motherly influence over a daughter: "But when Herod's birthday was kept, the daughter of Herodias danced before them, and pleased Herod. Whereupon he promised with an oath to give her whatsoever she would ask. And she, being before instructed of her mother, said, Give me here John Baptist's head in a charger" (Matthew 14:6-8).

But a mother can also have a godly influence: "When I call to remembrance the unfeigned faith that is in thee, which dwelt first in thy grandmother Lois, and thy mother Eunice; and I am persuaded that in thee also" (II Timothy 1:5).

An epitaph on the headstone of a woman's grave, though few in words, speaks volumes about her life: "Here Lies Our Sunshine."

The Bible presents the ideal for a wife and mother: "Strength and honour are her clothing; and she shall rejoice in time to come. She openeth her mouth with wisdom; and in her tongue is the law of kindness. She looketh well to the ways of her household, and eateth not the bread of idleness. Her children arise up, and call her blessed; her husband also, and he praiseth her" (Proverbs 31:25-28).

This is the type of mother and wife all women want to be. But it does not happen easily; a person has to work at it. Some days are not quite so bad, but others . . . they would be best forgotten. And the children do not seem to understand that they could make the job a lot easier. Although it is not easy, becoming a successful wife and mother is possible, and the rewards are many and precious.

Conclusion

A home is like the old capitol of the state of Kentucky, which is open to tourists. Most intriguing about this Greek revival structure is a curved, double, free-standing marble stairway. It is unique. Each carved step is interlocked with the one below and above it with no support other than the interlocked steps themselves. If any one step would be removed, the entire stairway would come crashing to the floor.

We can view the home in much the same light: both the husband and the wife are interlocked supports for the home structure. Each role is like a step in the free-standing staircase. If one is removed it threatens the disaster of the whole. We must not take chances, for the cost is too great. We must fulfill our support role wholeheartedly: keep from falling, hold up, give strength, encourage, provide, maintain, keep up, keep going, be in favor of, back, help, prove, bear out, endure (especially with patience or fortitude), bear, tolerate, assist, and protect!

5

Adding a Nursery

*I*n planning a nursery in a house, there is usually a bit of uncertainty. What color should it be—pink or blue? Should the decor be baby dolls or baseballs? For most, this uncertainty continues until the doctor's announcement in the delivery room. The news of expectancy is often greeted with "Do you want a boy or girl?" Most have a preference, and many make predictions.

Gender is only the beginning of the hopes and wishes that parents have for a child—hair color, eye color, health, personality, and so on. We cannot predetermine these matters, but there are many aspects of our children's lives and character in which we have great influence.

With a newborn comes a miniature library of free literature to help the parents care for the child. Any local library has volumes on child rearing, and the pediatrician's office supplies the parent with numerous brochures on the subject. Grandparents overflow with child-rearing wisdom. Still, the task at times seems overwhelming;

nothing seems to work. Why? Because each child is unique. This uniqueness refuses to fit into all the categorized molds that children are supposed to fit into. There are general truths that apply to all children, but all children do not fit all generalities. This truth is evident even in prenatal development. The standard length is nine months, but some babies come early and others late. The mom-to-be does not walk into the hospital on the 266th day and announce to the registrar that her baby is coming today. Rather, she waits for the baby to announce the arrival.

This chapter will not suggest a ninety-nine-step format for raising a standard child. Neither will it repeat the many excellent volumes on child rearing. Rather, the chapter will offer some insights that each parent can adapt for rearing a unique child.

Concept I:
The Parent Has the Primary Responsibility

Your child is your responsibility. Though this thought may have a negative connotation, it is a positive statement. At times other people may try to fulfill parental responsibilities—doctors, teachers, grandparents, church, day care, and government. These all have responsibilities to the child, and we appreciate the expertise and help they give, but no one should usurp parental responsibilities.

The child is a product of the parents. We must not overlook the unique parent-child love bond, which exists naturally. It is the unique design of our Creator. Natural parental love is tremendously powerful. With this in mind, it is quite evident that responsibility belongs with the parent, for no one else in all the world cares for a child like a parent is designed to care. Though many parents, for various reasons, neglect to care for a child, they are an unnatural exception to the rule. Their natural love has been altered by various circumstances and sins.

The child also has a love for the parents, but this love is different from the parents' love for the child. Were it not so, the child would choose to remain home with the parents forever. But the love of child for parent permits the child to leave home eventually and start another home. Parents, however, find it much harder to let the child go.

A conscientious judge often finds it difficult to take a child from natural parents. He understands that to break this bond of love can sometimes be more harmful to the child than the adverse circumstances of the home.

When we understand that responsibility for the child belongs to the parent, we can be a better parent for our child than any other person, institution, or influence. This concept helps to remove fear, doubt, and feelings of in-adequacy. Though we may not be experts in all areas of child rearing, we can be the best in raising our child. Though day-care activists herald the advantages of trained sitters for our children, especially in areas of education and socialization, after years of study many experts have now concluded that the parent-child love bond is far more important than for the child to know his ABC's before entering kindergarten.

Concept II: Concentrate on Needs

Too often parents confuse a child's needs and wants. His needs are basic, but like adults, his wants are unlimited. The wise parent will concentrate on the needs. They include love, physical care, discipline, and training.

Love

As mentioned earlier, nature provides a parent-child love bond. But adverse situations and stresses of life can affect this relationship. When a mother has to wash five loads of laundry, prepare three meals a day, clean up afterwards, vacuum, shop for groceries, and in the case of nearly one-half of the mothers of preschoolers, work outside the home, love can sometimes seem like an added chore.

For this reason, parents should give attention to cultivating the parent-child bond. As parents, we must sometimes reevaluate our priorities. Chores, schedules, jobs, and budgets must not take priority over inter-personal family relationships. We need to cultivate love and express it by communication, time spent together, and concern for little and big things such as a bruised knee or a broken toy. As an example, my two-year-old son came running into the house crying, "Mommy, come quick. There's a dead worm outside." My wife questioned, "How do you know it's dead?" He explained, "It doesn't have arms or legs." Such concerns shouldn't be brushed aside with "Oh, that's silly" or "I don't have time for such foolishness." Rather they are excellent opportunities for cultivating the parent-child love bond. Whether it is a young child worried about a dead worm, or a teenager who has just "fallen in love," parents must learn to lay "things" aside and cultivate the parent-child bond of love.

Physical Care

Physical care covers a wide range of matters including cleanliness, protection, clothing, nutritional meals, and health care (dental checkups, eye exams, physicals). Of course, this list is not exhaustive of the physical needs. As parents we should do all we can for our children's care, but various circumstances, namely finances, offer limitations. Without feeling guilty, we must place priorities on basic care first. Eyeglasses usually take priority over braces, nutritional foods must come before "goodies," and clothes before toys. Services through health clinics are sometimes available to those with limited finances. Though some are embarrassed to use such services, the care of the child needs to supersede our emotions.

Procrastination regarding physical care can be dangerous. Some things must not be put off, for serious damage is often the consequence. Poor eyesight or hearing loss can cause a host of other problems. Some physical problems, if detected in time, can be reversed.

Discipline

Too often, parents do not discipline a child until they are angry. At other times, they may neglect discipline simply because they hate to punish their children. But when we consider what discipline is for, and proper ways of disciplining, we can readily understand its value in child rearing. Discipline, though often called punishment, should be viewed more as a means of correction and training. When it is administered correctly, it will not only point out the improper offense committed, but it will also teach the proper action that the child should take in the future. Punishment alone simply expresses the parent's displeasure, and the child is often unaware of the reason. Likewise, if spanking is administered too often, without love, and in anger, then it can have reverse effects of what was intended. The Scriptures admonish parents to use "the rod" (physical discipline), but it is important to learn how to be effective in the administration of this form of discipline.

Discipline needs to incorporate love, firmness, consistency, swiftness, and fairness. There needs to be a balance of love and firmness. Love alone can produce a spoiled child, while firmness alone can produce a rebellious child. A parent should also be consistent. The child needs to know that discipline will not be sporadic. Discipline must not be a side effect of parental moods, nor should the parents allow wrongs to slip by because they are in a good mood. Discipline should be immediate or as near to the wrongdoing as possible, or else the child (especially the young one) may forget why he is being disciplined. But a parent should respect a child by not disciplining him in front of peers. The mother should not always wait for the father to come home from work to demand that he do something about the child's attitude; both parents must take the responsibility for discipline when appropriate. Discipline should be in proportion to the offense. Spanking is not necessary for a child who accidentally spills his milk, but it would be appropriate to have the child clean up the mess. When correction is administered with love, firmness, consistency, swiftness, and fairness, a lot less of it will be needed.

Training

Our approach to training needs to be holistic. We should consider that the child has physical, mental, social, and spiritual needs. Physical training includes activities such as exercise, fishing, sewing, doing chores, and riding a bicycle. Children sometimes refuse to participate in certain things simply because they have never been taught how. Emotional training includes developing an inner positive attitude about self. Social training includes learning to relate to others at home, school, work, and play. Some children, due to introverted natures, will need more attention in this area. A child who has difficulty in making friends should be encouraged, and special care can help the child make friends.

Spiritually, a child needs to be trained in the way of the Lord. This responsibility should not be left solely to the church. The parent needs to be totally involved. It is amazing how many parents will allow a child to skip church for fear he will get sick from lack of proper rest, yet send him off to school the next morning while he is half asleep for fear he will suffer academically. Or they may allow him to stay home from school because he is sick but let him go to the church hay ride in the evening.

Training must be properly balanced. A child needs to be prepared for heaven yet also trained for life on earth. As children grow up, exposure to improper influences outside the home can be damaging. Strong, supportive, parental influence can offset such detrimental influences. Here are some suggestions to enhance the parents' godly influence to "train up a child in the way he should go" (Proverbs 22:6).

1. *Be a committed parent.* Since parenting is a tiring job with many disappointments, you need commitment to propel you through the rough times. Patience is truly a virtue.

2. *Teach your child responsibility.* Many parents find it easier to do chores for their child rather than to take the time to train the child to do the chores. One mother

worked a job during the day, yet allowed her two teenage boys to watch idly as she mowed the grass and performed all the household tasks in the evening. An older son has been married now for two years and has yet to get a job. He is quite satisfied to allow his pregnant wife to provide for him. Childhood training definitely carries over into adulthood.

3. *Communicate.* Take time to listen, no matter how trivial the conversation. This establishes a pattern that the child will follow when he really needs someone to talk with.

4. *Build confidence and self-esteem in your child by offering positive remarks and praise for his efforts.* Offer suggestions in a positive manner rather than using negative criticism. For example, say, "I think you look very nice wearing your blue tie with that suit," instead of, "That red tie makes you look like a clown." Say, "I'm pleased with you for passing that math test." If necessary, at a later time you can suggest, "I think you can do better in math if you study a little more," instead of, "You idiot, another C! Why don't you get down to business?"

5. *Trust your child.* Parents should not create false guilt in a child by displaying a lack of trust, such as by third-degree questioning on everything the child does, everywhere he goes, and everyone he is with. This is not to suggest that you put your head in the sand and exhibit blind trust. That approach is foolish and will be quickly recognized by any child. Since you cannot place your child in a sterile, sin-free room until he is twenty-one, train him in the way he should go, provide strong parental support, and then believe in the child and his ability to do right.

6. *Instill respect.* You can do so by showing respect

to the child. For example, knock before entering his bedroom door and deliver him mail unopened. Strong rebuke should be done in private instead of in front of his peers.

7. *Forgive.* All children make errors. A parent must be quick to forgive and direct them in the right way. Forgiveness is important for three reasons. First, your children need your love. Second, you set an example for them to follow in forgiveness. Third, they can better understand and accept the forgiveness of Jesus Christ.

Concept III: Children Sometimes Go Astray

Though this concept is heartbreaking to parents, it is something we need to understand. When a child goes astray, the natural response of parents tends to be "Where did I go wrong?" But the best of parents must understand that children have a freedom of choice. Cain and Abel grew up under the same roof, with the same parents, and heard the same lectures. The Scripture does not fault Adam and Eve for Cain's sinful life. It was rather a matter of personal choice. But, like Job of old, we can continue to pray for our children and live a Christian example for them to follow.

Children reach an age in life when parents can only offer directions; the road children eventually take is a personal choice. Some people mistakenly interpret Proverbs 22:6 to mean that a child can never depart from parental teachings when he is old, a teaching that borders on eternal security. But godly training does not guarantee salvation for a child, although it certainly helps the odds. But, though a child chooses sin, it is very unlikely that he will ever erase the echoes of proper training from godly parents. Many factors can contribute to a child's choice, but the decision is ultimately the child's.

Proverbs 23:26 reads, "My son, give me thine heart, and let thine eyes observe my ways." There a righteous father pleaded for his son to follow his teaching and example. The Scriptures emphasize not only parental responsibility but also the decision of the child. A true story illustrates this point clearly. Two brothers, Bob and Jeff, were raised in the home of a father and stepmother. The stepmother made the home almost unbearable for both boys. Eventually, Jeff became bitter toward his parents and the church he had attended for years. In contrast, Bob remained respectful at home and found refuge in his church. He remains a faithful member of the church many years later. The difference in the brothers was their personal choices.

We must not excuse parental neglect by citing a child's personal choice, however. Instead, we should maintain close communication with our children in the area of biblical training. They should not only know the rules, but they should also have a scriptural understanding of the rules. Early in their academic training they will be taught to question, and they need an explanation other than "That's what we believe." The belief needs scriptural reinforcement. Not every rule or teaching is as plain or as authoritative as the Ten Commandments. But when we carefully explain the Scriptures, the child will be able to understand. For example, the Scripture does not say, "Thou shalt not smoke," but a host of verses teach the importance of keeping the body pure. The child should be taught the rule, but the rule should be reinforced by a scriptural explanation.

Too often parents stop short of this method of teaching. They may train the child to obey, using scripture for their rule, but then lay out all the rules without reinforcing them scripturally. What they often produce is children who obey rules only because they fear their parents. As they grow older, parental authority decreases and peer pressure increases, and eventually they become independent. They have a list of rules without a scriptural basis for following the rules.

Why do parents sometimes fail to train children properly? Doing so is a time-consuming job. Their schedule may be so filled with paying bills, cleaning house, shopping, working, and a thousand other things that they often do not take time to train their children.

As Apostolics, we cannot assume that our children will grow up to automatically accept what we believe. Rather, we must heed the command of the Lord: "And thou shalt teach them diligently unto thy children, and thou shalt talk of them when thou sittest in thine house, and when thou walkest by the way, and when thou liest down, and when thou riseth up" (Deuteronomy 6:7).

Concept IV: Learn to Turn Children Loose

After the parental responsibility of training is finished, somewhere around the child's early twenties, the parent must let go of the child. This release should not occur abruptly, however; it is a process that begins early in the child's life. From the beginning the parents should plan to develop an independent, well adjusted, socially responsible Christian child. The child will make mistakes that deeply hurt not only him but the parent also, and there is no guarantee that the child will meet parental expectations, but the parents must turn him loose.

Adjusting to the adult child's independence can be as difficult as parenting. At this point, the parents still feel responsible but sense the child no longer wants or needs their training. Too often they push the panic button prematurely and think the worst about anything and everything.

Parenting does not abruptly end on the child's eighteenth birthday or wedding day, but it goes through stages of transition. Though each stage is filled with uncertainty, we can adjust, ascertain proper goals, and fulfill our God-ordained role as parents. As from its beginning, parenting continues with many uncertainties, for the road is not perfectly mapped; it is one we chart and pave as we go. What a challenge!

But that is what makes parenting so personally rewarding. It is a personal, unique adventure. Happy and exciting traveling!

Home Repairs

Real estate is usually an excellent investment. On the one hand, a house ages and deteriorates. On the other hand, it usually appreciates in value. For a credit rating we say, "My house is worth much more than it cost me." That is true, if we have consistently kept it in repair.

And so we work diligently to keep the house in good repair. The passing viewers take a second look at the new roof or painted shutters, and they are indeed impressed. But what is the house like when we look beyond the cosmetic improvements, the thin veneer we portray to the public? What is it like inside the walls? Is there laughter and love or loneliness and longing? The family living in the house is more important than the dwelling. Keeping the house alone in good repair will only help the budget when the marriage partners split up.

The thought of divorce is disheartening, but it is a real possibility in our world. Marilynn Mansfield wrote in an article entitled "It Takes More Than the Wedding Ceremony to Make a Good Marriage That Will Last":

Confident that they are beginning a lifelong love affair, brides and bridegrooms exchange solemn vows. Unfortunately, demographers predict that one out of every two of the couples marrying this year will become a divorce statistic before their seventh wedding anniversary.

On the brighter side, newlyweds or longer-time marrieds can improve the odds, say the experts, by learning communication and decision-making skills. In time, with the right attitude and hard work, it even may be possible to turn around an older marriage gone sour.[1]

Neglected home (family) repairs are costly, for they cause division and misunderstandings. Walls of silence separate husband, wife, and children; the family room becomes a fighting ring; and meals have to be warmed twice and thrice for all to eat. The home becomes a boardinghouse, the mother a servant, the father a tyrant or at best a stranger, and the children demanding burdens. This situation does not have to be.

A house, whether new or old, is in constant need of maintenance. Repairs are part of the price for owning a house. Walls will crack, carpets wear thin, shingles blow off, paint fades, and appliances fail. Time and circumstances have a way of leaving their mark.

The same is true with the family. Every day brings the possibility of failure, broken trusts, cutting words, cracked relationships, challenged authority, fears, frustrations, anxieties, disappointments, misunderstandings, sickness, emotional distress, disagreements, exposed partiality, mounting bills, unexpected setbacks, and conflicting schedules. All of these problems demand immediate attention. They do not repair themselves. We must roll up our sleeves and get to work.

Too many times the need is met with neglect. The outcome is predictable, another seven-year statistic. But why? How can love be treated with such negligence? The answer is that neglect is seldom planned; often it begins with the smallest of problems. It happens because we are careless when repairs need to be made. There are at least four reasons why homes (marriages) deteriorate: lack of awareness, procrastination, unanticipated circumstances, and refusal to repair.

Lack of Awareness

From my teen years until I left home, I lived with my folks just across the river from Cincinnati. It was a real neat place—or at least I thought so. Concrete yards led from the street to our front door. We could mow the lawn in about five minutes with a pair of scissors. The rest we hosed off into the gutter. Every house boasted its personal paved playground, the street. The architect was amazing. He was able to design all the houses on the block just alike. And he did not believe in wasting space. Each house was built about three feet apart. When the house next to ours became vacant, my sister crawled from a second-story window of our house, across some wooden planks, and through an open window of the vacant house.

The city fathers were very generous also. They allowed us to purchase a ten-dollar permit so that we could park our car on the street in front of our house—on a first-come-first-served basis, of course. For convenience, every block had its own tavern. Main Street boasted many so-called adult entertainment centers.

I left home at the age of eighteen to attend Bible college. When I returned, everything had changed. How ugly the unswept gutters looked! The row of houses on my block had aged terribly. Everything appeared dull and run down. But the community really had not changed; I had.

After viewing other cities in various states, I had become more aware of the condition of my own. My perspective became focused with reality. My city was in much need of repairs. Oh, at one time it was indeed impressive, but time, circumstances, and neglect had eroded the urban beauty that it once possessed. We, the residents, had become so accustomed to our lifestyle and surroundings that we really did not notice all its flaws. Many of the houses needed painting. All the yards were small. Few homes could boast a garage. We had complacently compared ourselves with one another, giving ourselves passing grades. We knew nothing better.

This account is a good analogy of some families. Many families today have accepted a collision course of neglect. Since some parents came from homes in which the parents fussed and fought and the children were slapped and scolded constantly, they may accept this lifestyle as normal. After all, it was the way Mom and Dad did it. Some people look at other families who reflect failures similar to theirs and justify their own hostile actions or resign themselves to fate, saying, "This is the way it is supposed to be." Their senses have been dulled, and they are unaware of the failing condition of their home. In such situations children and parents typically seek ways of escape instead of remedies. "Countless studies show that misbehavior, poor academic performance, promiscuity, and drug and alcohol use often are manifestations of anger

100

over problems in the home."[2] They fail to understand that their home can and should be repaired.

Abigail Van Buren wrote, "Show me a married couple who boast that they have never had an argument and I'll show you a pair of love birds complete with bird-brains." There is no perfect marriage, but there are imperfect people striving to have a successful marriage. Success comes through an awareness of faults and failures and diligent efforts to improve and correct. The Bible does not teach that humans attain absolute perfection in this life, but it certainly points us in the direction of perfection. Abraham was ninety-nine years old when the Lord said to him, "Walk before me, and be thou perfect" (Genesis 17:1). He was ninety-nine years old and he had not reached perfection! But God was saying, "Here is the right road to take." All along life's road God posts directional signs: yield, slow down, danger, men working, curve, do not pass, stop.

Like Abraham, we can never claim to have "arrived" in this journey of perfection. A beautiful flower garden will become a weed patch without consistent care. Because we replaced a bad roof with a new one does not mean the roof will never leak again. If we overcome a petty jealousy or control our temper today, we must not sit back and rest on our laurels. Good home maintenance requires consistent evaluation, repair, and re-repair.

Procrastination

Some improvements go undone because of procrastination. We fully intend to make the repairs, when we get around to it. Procrastination proved to be disastrous to our house about three years ago. My wife,

Nancy, had asked me for some time to give much-needed attention to the latches on some of the windows. Our house was seventy-five years old and boasted thirteen large rooms on three floors. Unique lead-paned windows swung open inwardly. Age had worn some of the brass latches to the point that extreme winds would work the latches up and the windows would blow open. Disaster struck during the Christmas holiday.

We were out of state for several days visiting family in Ohio. On a windy, subzero day during our absence, a third-floor window blew open. The frigid air rushed into an upstairs bathroom, freezing the water lines and causing six breaks. Water gushed, running profusely for two days and making its way from the third floor to the basement. Ceilings collapsed, beautiful hardwood flooring buckled, and swollen doors would not close. When we returned, smoke filled the house from smoldering electrical wires. Furniture and personal belongings were damaged, and some were ruined. But this was only the beginning. Ahead of us was a complete year of living in frustration due to plumbers, painters, cleaners, carpenters, carpet layers, wallpaper hangers, insurance adjusters, the curious, and the constant mess. All of this was the result of procrastination, neglect, being too busy, an "I'll do it next week" attitude. One nail could have prevented it all.

Likewise, there are some problems in the home that must not wait. Procrastination prolongs frustration and often creates bigger problems. The rebellious attitude of a child must be tended to today. The seemingly simple rebellion may be an indication that a much bigger storm is brewing. A child may be having problems with drugs, premarital sex, guilt, or fears about the future. Misunderstandings between spouses cannot wait until deer season is over. The deer stand will not keep a man warm on a long, wintry night. The budget cannot continue unbalanced. A family must not keep putting off much needed family prayer. To have problems is normal, but to procrastinate in solving life's problems is inexcusable.

Some problems seem impossible to correct. They are, if we never start trying. As we walked into the house that very wet Christmas, our hearts sank with despair, shock, and disbelief. I sat down on a stairway staring in utter dismay. It was like sitting in a rainstorm, for water was pouring from the ceiling. I was drenched. Nancy took one look and rushed into the kitchen. She grabbed pans and waste cans and started placing them around the room to catch the water. Her hair was plastered to her head, and water ran down her face. I shook my head. It was hopeless. "Turn off the main water line!" she barked. "Get some towels! Rent a wet vac!" "It's too late," I argued. All her little efforts seemed so futile in the mess that we were facing, but they were the beginning to a solution to our dilemma. We had to start somewhere and right away!

When a person sees a needed home repair, it is time to get to work. It is not the time to crawl off into the corner and lick sores of self-pity. We must fight against feeling overwhelmed. For every problem, God offers a solution. He will not slap us in the face with it, however; He expects us to use some initiative. If a couple feels that they cannot tackle the problem alone, they should seek spiritual guidance, sharing their struggles with a wise and trusted friend who can offer some help.

The Middle East offers an illustration of the danger of procrastination. The land on the east side of the Jordan River and the land on the west side of the Jordan are vastly different. Israel, the western part, though extremely hot, is planted with various crops. Workers pump water from the north to the thirsty southern fields. They have planted trees on the barren hillsides. Reasoning that nature supplies the need for water, they contend that planting trees has caused more rainfall to be retained rather than unnecessarily using the small amount of rainfall. Procrastination is not in their vocabulary, but they create, solve, rectify, and work. The land has blossomed under that philosophy.

A tour guide pointed out the vast contrast between the two banks. The land to the east of the Jordan River is barren, treeless, and virtually useless. The guide suggested the inhabitants' philosophy is, "If God wants to bless the land, He will. If He wants to send rain, we will accept it. But there is no need for us to do anything. We cannot change fate."

By contrast, the Israelis say, "God has given me a brain. He expects me to use it. If I fail to use it, to act, to initiate, or plan for the future, God will not bless my apathy. He will bless my efforts." Though this example may reflect a biased opinion, it is a good analogy of procrastination versus action.

In many scriptural accounts, perhaps the outcome would have been different if people had not procrastinated. Let us consider Lot. Did he sense earlier that Sodom was not a proper place for raising a family? What if he had tackled the problem immediately? Would his entire family have been saved? Or King David, did he neglect young Absalom's rebellious childhood, intending to have a father-son talk with him after he had taken care of other problems in his empire? What about Felix, when he heard the witness of the apostle Paul? "And as he reasoned of righteousness, temperance, and judgment to come, Felix trembled, and answered, Go thy way for this time; when I have a convenient season, I will call for thee" (Acts 24:25). Did procrastination keep Felix out of heaven?

If there is a flaw that Satan can capitalize on, it is procrastination. While we hesitate, he connives, plots, accuses, and confuses the issue at hand. At the end of our procrastination, when we finally decide to act, we have a much bigger problem than when we first recognized it.

Unanticipated Circumstances

It is impossible to make a house exempt from misfortune. Plan as we may, it is still susceptible to fire, tornado, flood, lightning, failed electricity, and earthquake. Some houses have been gobbled up overnight by giant sink holes. Others were built over an area of land that holds a poisonous gas deep in the earth's surface. The deadly gas is escaping and seeping into the houses. Tests are now under way to determine what other houses are built over these dangerous conditions.

In another tragic example, the townspeople of a southern Indiana community felt safe and secure in their serene setting. They were far removed from big-city smog and pollution, or at least they thought so. Then came the horrid news: a chemical dump was located within their city limits. A business had improperly stored chemical wastes on its property for many years. The containers holding the chemicals were leaking the toxics into the ground. Consequently, the poison had contaminated the water supply. The cleanup will take years; the total damage remains unknown until it is revealed in the health of those exposed to the chemicals through the water. It is impossible to build a house totally immune from unwanted or unanticipated circumstances.

The same is true of the family. Unplanned, unexpected, and adverse circumstances occur in any marriage. One husband explains, "Early in our marriage we experienced three unexpected circumstances in one week. My wife found out she was going to have a baby, which meant a job change for her, my car broke down, and we were asked to move. Our landlady gave us one week to relocate, which she felt was plenty of time. We were young, inexperienced, and a thousand miles from home. It seemed like the end. Sixteen years later we realized that was the beginning of our education on real life. Now we try to tackle each problem with wisdom, much prayer, and bulldog determination. We keep hammer, nails, and paintbrush on hand, along with a continuing account at the hardware store."

Let us examine some unanticipated circumstances.

Children

A couple's response to finding out that they are going to have a child, planned or not, is usually twofold: joy and anxiety. They may think, We want a child, but now? How will we pay the doctor bill? We do not have a nursery; our second income will be terminated; and how can we afford baby clothes, Pampers, and a car seat?

Though most prospective parents experience these initial emotions, some do not learn how to handle them.

One young man blamed his wife entirely for the pregnancy and would not speak to her for two weeks upon receiving the news. Too often a person dumps his bucket of frustration on the one dearest to him, his spouse, who in turn responds adversely, and soon there is an all-out war. This is especially sad when it happens because a baby, whom both love dearly, has interrupted plans.

Phil and Ruth had applied for technical training in St. Louis when they realized their family was going to increase. Ruth had to give up furthering her education for a while, and Phil had to finish his sooner than planned so they could resettle before the birth. Were they disappointed? Probably, but they accepted the necessary changes without turmoil in their relationship.

Incompatibility

The time, planning, efforts, and money put into a wedding are all indications of the couple's intent to live "till death do us part." Robert Taylor explains why this expectation sometimes fails:

> Each assumes the union will last forever. Yet, as the years pass, the partners often drift apart. Sometimes the gulf is widened by physical abuse, mental cruelty, or blatant infidelity. But more often, the husband and wife grow from lovers to opponents. It doesn't happen overnight. Day by day, small disagreements escalate into continuing warfare, and soon the home becomes a battlefield. From time to time a truce is attempted, but hostilities soon break out again.[3]

Incompatibility results from an inexorable attitude

on the part of one or both partners. The longer a person remains inflexible, the more difficulty he will experience in reaching a peaceful relationship. It is each spouse's obligation to be willing to go at least halfway. Why would anyone feel that he should have everything his way? Marriage is to be a blending of two separate personalities into one union. Each must compromise, laying aside stubbornness and selfishness, to please the other. It is a shame for anyone to demand his or her own way all the time.

Any marriage can be salvaged if both partners are willing to work toward a solution. The circumstances causing the wedge must be mutually acknowledged. If this is not possible, perhaps the partners are too close to the forest to see the trees, and they should seek impartial spiritual counsel. A wise pastor can help uncover the root of the problem. Renewal begins by asking forgiveness of God and each other, and it continues with much prayer.

One couple felt their marriage was over. The wife claimed that her husband had destroyed her love for him. After rededication to God, their spirits softened toward one another. Somehow it was no longer so distasteful to prefer the other's wishes. Later, the wife ecstatically testified that God not only renewed her love for her husband, but she loved him more than she ever had. Many years have passed and they are still married.

For many, divorce seems the easiest solution. It is not. Unless adultery is involved, divorce is scripturally out of the question. Paul wrote to the Corinthians, "And unto the married I command, yet not I, but the Lord, let not the wife depart from her husband: but and if she depart, let her remain unmarried, or be reconciled to her husband: and let not the husband put away his wife" (I Corinthians 7:10-11).

First, we need to realize that this command comes from the Lord. Paul cited the teaching of Jesus Himself. (See Mark 10:1-12; Luke 16:18.) Moreover, God inspired Paul to write these words. Though the Old Testament law recognized divorce (Deuteronomy 24:1), God was not pleased with divorce even then (Malachi 2:14-16). He merely tolerated it as an alternative to protect wives. In Old Testament times, husbands typically had power to divorce their wives almost at will, with little or no provisions for her, or they could marry multiple wives. Deuteronomy 24:1-4 sought to regulate and minimize the wrong. Commenting on this provision Jesus said, "For the hardness of your heart he [Moses] wrote you this precept. But from the beginning of the creation God made them male and female. For this cause shall a man leave his father and mother, and cleave to his wife; and they twain shall be one flesh; so then they are no more twain, but one flesh. What therefore God hath joined together, let not man put asunder" (Mark 10:5-9).

Second, Paul commanded the wife not to depart from her husband. Paul did not want the wife to leave her husband, but rather he wanted the couple to work out their differences.

Third, let us notice two words in verse 11: *but* and *if*. "But and if she depart, let her remain unmarried." Since some situations are extremely unpleasant—such as cases of physical abuse—Paul did not bind the wife to the same house with the man, but he left her an alternative. If she must leave, she has two options: "remain unmarried, or be reconciled to her husband."

Fourth, Paul explicitly commanded the husband not to "put away" (divorce) his wife. Incompatibility is no excuse for divorce. Instead, the marriage should be reconciled.

Incompatibility often arises when only one of the marriage partners gets saved. The marriage originally incorporated certain non-Christian ideas and practices such as going to movies, dancing, worldly parties, sinful habits, and so on. Since the Christian no longer wants to participate in these things, the marriage can quickly run aground. Paul gave inspired instruction for such a circumstance, which Jesus had not specifically addressed:

But to the rest speak I, not the Lord: If any brother hath a wife that believeth not, and she be pleased to dwell with him, let him not put her away. And the woman which hath an husband that believeth not, and if he be pleased to dwell with her, let her not leave him. For the unbelieving husband is sanctified by the wife, and the unbelieving wife is sanctified by the husband: else were your children unclean; but now are they holy. But if the unbelieving depart, let him depart. A brother or a sister is not under bondage in such cases: but God hath called us to peace. For what knowest thou, O wife, whether thou shalt save thy husband? or how knowest thou, O man, whether thou shalt save thy wife? (I Corinthians 7:12-16).

Paul first emphasized for the marriage to continue. God still acknowledges the marriage even though it is between an unbeliever and a believer. By staying, the believer has a sanctifying influence upon the children. Moreover, it is hoped that the believer will win the unbeliever to the Lord, which is a great reason for the marriage to continue.

Here are some guidelines for living with an unbelieving spouse and helping to convert him or her.

1. *Do not preach to your spouse.* Let your witness be
mostly by example. As time passes he or she will ask direct
questions that will offer opportunity to witness.

2. *Do not exalt the minister too much.* Jealousy is
often the result.

3. *Be patient and continue to live a consistent Christian life before your spouse.* "Likewise, ye wives, be in
subjection to your own husbands; that, if any obey not
the word, they also may without the word be won by the
conversation of the wives; while they behold your chaste
conversation coupled with fear" (I Peter 3:1-2).

4. *Pray earnestly for your spouse.* Have another
believer of your sex to believe with you in prayer for the
salvation of your spouse. "Again I say unto you, That if
two of you shall agree on earth as touching any thing that
they shall ask, it shall be done for them of my Father
which is in heaven" (Matthew 18:19).

5. *Express your love for your spouse.* He or she may
feel threatened by the church. Give the assurance that
you are happy to be married to your spouse.

6. *Don't give an ultimatum unless it is impossible to
live under the circumstances.* If you say, "Either you get
saved or we're through," you may be partially responsible for ending a marriage contrary to God's will.

7. *Do not entertain thoughts of divorce.* The only scriptural ground for divorce is adultery, although other circumstances make it dangerous or impossible for the
believer to stay with the spouse. Of course, if the
unbeliever chooses to leave, the believer cannot prevent
the departure and has no obligation to follow after the

departed spouse. "But if the unbelieving depart, let him depart. A brother or a sister is not under bondage in such cases: but God hath called us to peace" (I Corinthians 7:15).

One son testified, "My dad is a beautiful example of a Christian witness to an unsaved spouse. He lived for God sixteen years before my mother or any of us seven children gave our hearts to the Lord. I am so grateful that he remained steadfast."

Infidelity

Few enter marriage with thoughts of infidelity. Marriage to most means forsaking all others and clinging only to one. Yet, by one estimate, one-half of all marriages in the United States will experience infidelity. Infidelity has to be the most difficult home repair to encounter. We do not have to think long to recall a Christian marriage that has entered into the divorce statistics because of this failure. Chapter 4 discussed basic principles to prevent infidelity in a marriage. Now let us address both the innocent and the guilty who have experienced the trauma of an extramarital affair.

Remorse fills the guilty with its crushing indictment. Guilt trails him like a bloodhound. There is no place to hide, no peace. Those who fall into this trap are not necessarily bad people. But whether committed out of foolishness or selfishness, adultery is still sin. Sincere repentance is necessary—sorrow for the sin and a turning away from it. There is forgiveness from the Lord. To King David, Nathan pronounced, "The LORD also hath put away thy sin; thou shalt not die" (II Samuel 12:13). Jesus said unto the adulterous woman, "Neither do I condemn thee: go, and sin no more" (John 8:11).

The big question for the guilty is, "Should I tell my spouse or keep it my secret?" A spouse may not want to hear the confession. Judy told her husband, "If you are ever unfaithful to me, please don't tell me." But then, what if the guilty party does not tell and the partner in a one-night fling does? It would be better for a wife or husband to hear it from a spouse than from someone else. Can a person bear the guilt without sharing it? Will it affect the marriage relationship adversely if not shared? These and more questions need to be given much thought. The one suggestion I offer is, Do not make a decision to tell without counsel. If the guilty party is considering telling the spouse, a qualified Christian counselor, preferably the pastor, can help the guilty party decide how best to handle the situation.

If the guilty party chooses to tell the spouse of the infidelity, he or she must be prepared for the mate's decision regarding the continuation of the marriage. The guilty party is not in a position to make any demands; adultery is scriptural grounds for divorce. A dozen red roses is not a magic, overnight cure-all.

The innocent spouse will go through various emotional stages, and they will take time. A decision must be made. Can the innocent mate forgive and accept the unfaithful mate? Or will the innocent one continue the marriage in a legal sense only, avoiding any future intimacies as a husband and wife? Ideally, the marriage will continue with forgiveness and a renewed pledge of faithfulness. Unless a final decision of divorce is made, the children should not be involved. If the marriage is saved, there is no reason for the children ever to know of the crisis. It is a burden they need not bear.

There are reasons for the marriage to continue. In most cases, divorce is not the best solution. The marriage can go on, not just legally, but with renewed commitment. A key factor must be involved, however: just as the initial marriage was an agreement between the two parties, so reconciliation of the marriage also requires an agreement between husband and wife. The innocent must be willing to forgive, and the guilty must be willing to repent and to accept forgiveness. Restoring confidence will be a process rather than an immediate decision. Time is essential for the healing of this deadly wound.

The innocent mate typically goes through the following states and must work through these emotions in order for healing to take place.

1. *Shock* or disbelief. "Surely it can't be. I never dreamed it could happen to our marriage." For days the innocent mate awakes to the hope that the infidelity was just a nightmare, but reality dashes salt into the raw wound of broken trust.

2. *Resentment, bitterness,* or even hate. The innocent may be tempted to get even, perhaps to the point of having an affair with a friend of the guilty spouse or remaining married with no intentions of ever forgiving but making the guilty pay for the wrong instead. Revenge may come in the form of constant reminders of the past, permanently refusing intimacy, or doing anything else to make the guilty person's life miserable.

3. *Guilt.* The innocent person cannot help but wonder if he or she caused the affair by not being a desirable marriage partner. The person questions, Did I neglect the needs of my spouse?

4. *Depression.* The innocent person dreads facing a

114

world full of questions, rumors, and gossip and is overwhelmed by heartache. He or she may even contemplate suicide as a quick way out.

5. *Acceptance.* The person must finally accept the fact that unfaithfulness has entered the marriage. He or she must determine what to do—to continue the marriage or to dissolve it. This decision requires serious prayer and Christian counsel, not just the counsel of a neighbor or relative. Yes, divorce is an option, but the consequences must be considered. How will a divorce affect the children? Statistics say children are usually the victims. How will the innocent person's own life be affectd? How will the community and the church be affected? What will a divorce do to a person's Christian witness? Is the guilty party truly willing to forsake evil and to work to restore the marriage? If a spouse has truly repented, forsaken the affair, and received the forgiveness of Jesus Christ, should a mate refuse to forgive? These are a few of the questions that need to be asked. With time, prayer, and spiritual counsel, the marriage can experience renewed love.

This discussion is not meant to suggest that a marriage be continued to simply avoid embarrassment, especially if the guilty party does not demonstrate repentance and a changed lifestyle. But a marriage should be continued on the basis that it is the right thing to do. If an unfaithful spouse realizes his or her wrong, sincerely seeks forgiveness from God and spouse, and renews the pledges of love, trust, and faithfulness, then the innocent person can genuinely love again.

6. *Healing.* It is foolish to say there will be no scar from the wound. But if each partner will seek to save the

marriage as aggressively as many seek to dissolve theirs, the marriage can be salvaged. The Adamic nature will rage, "Make the guilty bear the shame and the blame." The Spirit of Christ will nudge, "I forgave you all." Both the innocent and the guilty will have to let go of the past, live for the present and future, forgive, repair the home, shed their pride, and follow Christ.

Loss of Employment

Some of the most frightening words a man can hear are, "We no longer need your services. We're letting you go." For some this notice proves to be devastating, but for others it is a blessing. The initial shock is enough to jar any home, not to mention the havoc that it plays on the male ego.

One man, a very brilliant and capable high school teacher, went through a year of unemployment. He had been replaced because of a racial imbalance among the staff members. He responded as if he had been fired due to terrible ineptness. His self-esteem hit the bottom. He considered himself a failure and would not even try for another teaching position. He did one thing right, however: he kept his dedication to the Lord. He made it through the storm and eventually was hired by another school district. During this time, his wife worked and provided their income. Not once did she lose respect for her husband or mistreat him in any manner. Her support and confidence was a great aid in his healing process. For many men, this misfortune would have meant divorce. And yet it is something that many of us will face at least once in a lifetime.

Making friends and acquaintances aware of the

unemployment is wise. They will not pass on information regarding possible jobs if they are not aware of the circumstances. It is also important that the unemployed person not allow himself to become bored. If he does, depression will result. He must remain busy, continue to arise early, and aggressively seek new employment. A crisply typed resume and a neat appearance are assets. And while he waits on a job opening, he should help around the house and church. Perhaps now he will have the time to make neglected repairs. He can also take up an inexpensive hobby, read an inspiring book, plant a garden, spend more time in devotions, and be more involved in the ministries of the church.

The newly unemployed person should avoid pushing the panic button and selling the house. If he is forced to sell the house eventually, if at all possible he should save the equity for the purchase of another house later. The family may be able to cut back in other areas and leave their down payment money in the savings account.

This time can be a period of spiritual growth. One person related, "Before my father was able to receive disability assistance after his prolonged illness, he and my mother were forced to live without an income for one year. Dad testified, 'I have learned a lot about faith this year. In the past I relied on my own resourcefulness in providing for my family. This year I have learned what it means to trust in the Lord daily for our needs. Whenever there has been a need, God has miraculously supplied. All our bills have been paid on time, and there has always been food on the table. God is no respecter of persons. He will do the same for anyone who asks in faith. I am not referring to the lazy, immature husband who almost looks forward to the pink slip so that he can sleep late and receive unemployment checks and food stamps. I am talking about the honest, hard worker who is doing his best to take care of his family, but gets the boot unfairly.' "

The husband should sign up for deserved unemployment but immediately begin looking for a new job. There is a danger in becoming comfortable in the unemployed state. It may be necessary to accept another type of work temporarily, as well as a pay cut. Having a job will help him obtain a better position. Employers are skeptical of the unemployed, especially if they have been unemployed for some length of time. The important thing is not to become discouraged easily.

The wife's understanding and support are very important. Donna expressed, "My husband feels like he is not a man because he cannot provide for his family. I am partially to blame because I did not understand what he was feeling emotionally. I verbally condemned him for being out of work."

If hard times persist, local services are available and should be sought. The unemployed person has paid for this aid many times over in taxes, and therefore he should not regard it as charity. Regardless, it is not a shame to need help. One service available is job training, which can provide the opportunity to upgrade employment qualifications. A call to the local employment service is in order.

A job change may be best. Jeff was at first visibly shaken at the loss of his employment, but he later expressed that he was so glad to be out of the factory where he had to punch a time clock and into an insurance job that he thoroughly enjoyed.

Of course, God expects us to do our part and to pray, but we can rest assured that He takes care of His own.

Sickness

One man testified, "I became ill suddenly, which forced me to retire six years before I had planned. It never entered my mind that I would become disabled." Many people can relate to this story. Sickness is definitely an unplanned circumstance in a marriage. It can strike at any age. Often there is no repair or cure short of a miracle; rather, the family must learn to adjust. Daily habits, goals, and dreams undergo radical change.

Sometimes the afflicted spouse runs away or makes plans to do so. This action is the result of a lack of communication. The sick member feels he is a bother and no longer a benefit to the family. He may determine that it is too agonizing for the family to see him suffer and die. But the family suffers in worrying over the whereabouts of a loved one and blaming themselves for his decision to leave. The torture does not end there, for the family is left with a legal mess unless a body is found and properly identified. Insurance policies will go unclaimed, and the surviving spouse may lose social security benefits. The decision to run only creates more problems.

On the other hand some afflicted spouses become very selfish and make unrealistic demands on a mate. George would allow no one to take care of him other than his wife, and he begrudged her of any time away from the house. When she returned she was greeted with a tirade of questions regarding her absence: "Where did you go? Who did you talk with? Why did it take so long?" This type of behavior is unfair and causes a great deal of additional stress for the healthy mate.

How does a person accept illness? Only one who has been there can fully understand. Marie said she determined to make the best of each day and enjoy the companionship of her loved ones while she could. A key is keeping a pleasant frame of mind and looking for things for which to be thankful. When we look around us, beyond the walls of our distress, we can observe others who are suffering even greater difficulties. We may complain of poor eyesight until we meet a blind person who has never seen a sunset.

Each person has the choice of how to react to illness. Charlotte was diagnosed with cancer. She spent her days sharing God's love and peace with the hospital staff who attended her. Visitors left her bedside encouraged and cheered. Though in great pain she would smile and say, "I'm ready to go when the Lord calls me. I am not afraid."

No one is immune to the misfortune of illness. Both the young and the old are afflicted. Almost everyone will experience some type of unplanned, life-altering circumstance. When we realize that this life is but a vapor compared with eternity, it assures us even more that our ultimate goal has to be a life lived for Christ and the reward of eternal life in heaven.

Admittedly, someone's sickness may be burdensome to others, but true love remains in sickness and in health. That love will be expressed in the daily care given to the afflicted. The sick mate does not need to wallow in self-pity or guilt over the extra care the affliction causes, and he or she should accept help from a mate and family with a thankful heart. This thankfulness needs to be expressed.

One deeply moving story deals with the attitude with which a mother and her seven-year-old son accepted his blindness. She said, "Son, you may have lost your sight, but you still have your mind." He went on living, becoming famous and successful. Afflicted people still have love to give to a family, prayers to offer, a smile, and a witness to share. They can be an inspiration to everyone around them.

Even death is not to be feared. The memory of a deceased love one lives on in the hearts and minds of family and friends. And better still, death is the doorway to eternal life. It is the only thing that separates us from eternal bliss. Death for the believer is victory. "Death is swallowed up in victory. O death, where is thy sting? O grave, where is thy victory?" (I Corinthians 15:54-55). The departed saint has acquired what we all long for.

If you are one who must look after the sick, bear your lot graciously. Your attitude toward your responsibility will determine whether or not you do it willingly with a smile or grudgingly. Yes, it is a tiring responsibility. Our hats are off to the many who must bear this burden. Many people do not know the extra work involved in caring night and day for a sick spouse. But neither have they experienced the closeness that such care can bring. Make this time as pleasant as possible. Though your life will be altered, still you must continue to function as normally as possible: try to take a shopping trip, attend social gatherings, and so on. You will need someone to give you a break from time to time. Do not feel guilty that you can still enjoy these experiences but your mate cannot. Share them with your mate and try to make the absent one still feel a part. Continue to communicate outside the walls of your home.

Conclusion
These and a host of other circumstances can invade

the home. Though they may be unanticipated and though many cannot be prevented, they can be either corrected or adjusted to. The home need not be destroyed.

Here are several guidelines for handling the unanticipated:

1. *Communicate.* Give close attention to communication, as discussed in chapter 2. Share your feelings even though they may seem trivial, silly, or personal.

2. *Admit and agree on the need for repair.* What is the basic problem? Seek counsel when needed or to verify your conclusions. Realize that an overnight remedy may not exist.

3. *Form a plan of action.* It may include both spiritual and physical changes. You may have to purchase a one-floor house to eliminate climbing stairways, or move to a different climate. When for years you have traveled to church to receive spiritual direction and food, the church may now have to come to you.

4. *Follow your plan.*

5. *Reevaluate the situation periodically.* Make sure your plan is working. If it is not, start the process over with step 2.

Refusal to Repair

Some houses deteriorate because the owners refuse to put any time, effort, or money into much needed repairs. They live as if, poof! somehow it will all come together, as if it just needs a little time. They feel that the roof will automatically stop leaking, the faucet will quit dripping, the paint will cease chipping. They sound like the old-timer in a humorous story. When he was asked why he did not fix his leaking roof, he explained, "When

it is raining, I can't. And when it's sunny, I don't need
to." In reality, he never intends to.

A deteriorating house is sad, but a deteriorating home
is tragic. Yet some husbands and wives simply refuse to
repair. With an iron-fisted grip they cling to a stubborn
will. Phrases such as "It's all in his mind" or "She's just
like her mother" are the only excuses they need to stand
their ground. This is the attitude many take today, and
as a result the divorce lawyers are thriving.

Many people read advice on marriage but say, "I don't
have a problem. My spouse has the problem." But our
spouse's problem *is* our problem. One couple played this
game for years. "She's got the problem," he would say.
"There's really nothing wrong." They were both Christians, but he was blind to what he was doing wrong. He
never would acknowledge any fault or error on his part.
The result was tragic.

How much do you value your wife, or husband, or
children—your home? Priceless, you say? Then do not
neglect home repairs. Make sure the value of your home
continues to appreciate.

7

Finances

*A*ll building programs seem to have one thing in common: they cost more than originally planned. Unexpected price increases; broken, lost, or stolen materials; added features; and forgotten necessities quickly gobble up and exceed the planned budget.

The same is true with family finances. There is always the unexpected, the forgotten, and the added. Often these expenses come just when we think there is hope for our financial situation. Somehow we get our college loan paid just in time to start saving for our child's college education. Charles Swindoll states in his excellent book, *Strike the Original Match,* "Nine out of every ten people with an income are financial failures."[1] Tim and Beverly Lahaye say in *Spirit-Controlled Family Living,* "The basic problem in over 70 percent of the marriages that fail stems from finances."[2]

Money problems cause great strain in any marriage, triggering frustration that often leads to divorce court.

For a happy and enduring marriage, a couple must control the area of finances. We must not stumble into the pitfall of thinking what we need is more money. What we really need is a handle on the money we have. Failing to control our spending habits with the few dollars that we have is sure proof that we cannot control our spending habits with more money.

There are Christians who excel in many areas of life but are financial failures. They are unable to manage money. The changes in interest rates and the seesaw game of inflation keep them financially strapped. They have never quite been able to take charge of their finances. This failure is due largely to a lack of understanding of the general goals of financial planning, the lack of a plan to carry out objectives, and a lack of self-disciplinary action to keep on track with the plan.

People's view of money varies. Some work to get money. Others get money for their work. A friend of mine calls money "a necessary nuisance." I chuckle because he is well off financially. To some money is power, and for others it is security. Gordon McLean truly says, "Money is a wonderful servant, but a terrible master."[3] We must not be mastered by but be master over our money.

Our attitude about money is extremely important, as the Bible clearly teaches: "For the love of money is the root of all evil" (I Timothy 6:10). Money is not the root of all evil, but the love of money—an attitude about money—is the problem.

Many people who are wealthy are not happy. Solomon is a classic example:

I gathered me also silver and gold, and the peculiar treasure of kings and of the provinces: I gat me men singers and women singers, and the delights of the sons of men, as musical instruments, and that of all sorts. So I was great, and increased more than all that were before me in Jerusalem: also my wisdom remained with me. And whatsoever mine eyes desired I kept not from them, I withheld not my heart from any joy; for my heart rejoiced in all my labour: and this was my portion of all my labour. Then I looked on all the works that my hands had wrought, and on the labour that I had laboured to do: and, behold, all was vanity and vexation of spirit, and there was no profit under the sun (Ecclesiastes 2:8-11).

In contrast, others in spite of their poverty, are not sad. Paul learned this lesson well. "For I have learned, in whatsoever state I am, therewith to be content" (Philippians 4:11). That is the message of this chapter: not to show us how to get more, but how to enjoy more with what we already have.

Numerous circumstances can affect our income. A bright and promising career can be shattered by one unfortunate event. An income can go from six figures to unemployment overnight. Life is full of the unexpected. For example, several years ago my father experienced painful sores on his feet and legs. Reluctantly he went into the hospital for the first time in his life. Dad had worked hard all his life, seldom experiencing any type of sickness. He was shocked by the outcome of this sudden illness. He was never able to return to work and was forced to retire six years before his plans, with a drastic cut in income. Life is uncertain.

Though we cannot always control the amount of money we make, we *can* control our attitude about our money. Here are some simple guidelines to follow, whether someone makes ten thousand dollars a year or one hundred thousand:
Work hard.
Give liberally.
Spend wisely.
Save consistently.
Enjoy the reward.

Work Hard
The Bible is very clear on the subject of work. Let us consider some of the many passages of Scripture concerning its importance:

Go to the ant, thou sluggard; consider her ways, and be wise: which having no guide, overseer, or ruler, provideth her meat in the summer, and gathereth her food in the harvest. How long wilt thou sleep, O sluggard? when wilt thou arise out of thy sleep? Yet a little sleep, a little slumber, a little folding of the hands to sleep: so shall thy poverty come as one that travelleth, and thy want as an armed man (Proverbs 6:6-11).

Love not sleep, lest thou come to poverty; open thine eyes, and thou shalt be satisfied with bread (Proverbs 20:13).

For even when we were with you, this we commanded you, that if any would not work, neither should he eat. For we hear that there are some which walk among you dis-

orderly, working not at all, but are busybodies (II Thessalonians 3:10-11).

The Bible leaves no room for doubt; work is a command. But with the command comes a promise: "Thou shalt be satisfied with bread" (Proverbs 20:13). Bread represents all the sustenance for life. If we work, we will be satisfied. Along with a promise for those who work comes a warning for those who are too lazy to work: poverty.

What about those who get wealth dishonestly or accidentally? The Bible covers this area too: "Wealth gotten by vanity shall be diminished: but he that gathered by labour shall increase" (Proverbs 13:11). Recently a young man won a state lottery. He will receive $150,000 a year for twenty years. Surely his financial worries are over, someone may think, but not necessarily. He has already borrowed from next year's allowance. He has bypassed a vital part of life—work. He is prone to miss work's reward, enjoying the fruit of his labor.

Of course, there is also the workaholic. He usually succeeds financially but comes up short in areas of equal or greater importance. The children may have grown up and moved out of the home six weeks before he notices they are gone.

Whatever our occupation, we should work at it diligently. But what about those who do not like their job? Most of us will have to work a job we do not enjoy sometime in life. In this case, we should seek another job, but while we do, keep working hard on the job we have. It is a mistake to quit to find work. Employers prefer hiring the employed over the unemployed. They suspect the unemployed may be unemployed because of a lack of zeal for work.

God does not want us to be poor; He has said He would supply our needs. We are to be poor in spirit but not necessarily poor financially. Yet numerous Christians cannot make ends meet. Some may misinterpret Scripture to teach that poverty and spirituality are synonymous. True, some great Christians have lived a life of poverty, but the reason for their poverty was circumstances, not spiritual elevation. Neither poverty nor wealth is a sign of spirituality or unspirituality. God blesses His people materially, but His greatest blessings are not material.

Others view the Scriptures as teaching that God is obligated to bless us financially, whether we work hard or not at all. God's provision, however, is contingent upon whether or not we work. He blesses our endeavors, not our lack of them.

But simply working hard is no guarantee of financial success. It is merely a part of God's plan.

Give Liberally
The second part of God's financial plan is for us to give generously. Again, the Bible instructs us in this matter. Giving is a command, not merely optional. Obedience brings reward, while neglect brings judgment.

Will a man rob God? Yet ye have robbed me. But ye say, Wherein have we robbed thee? In tithes and offerings. Ye are cursed with a curse: for ye have robbed me, even this whole nation. Bring ye all the tithes into the storehouse, that there may be meat in mine house, and prove me now herewith, saith the LORD of hosts, if I will not open you the windows of heaven, and pour you out a blessing, that there shall not be room enough to receive it. And I will rebuke the devourer for your sakes, and he shall not destroy the fruits of your ground; neither shall your vine cast her fruit before the time in the field, saith the LORD of hosts. And all nations shall call you blessed: for ye shall be a delightsome land, saith the LORD of hosts (Malachi 3:8-12).

To please God we should give according to the following five principles, as listed in the words of Frank Charles Thompson:

- Give according to income.
- Give according to ability.
- Give without ostentation.
- Give regularly.
- Give cheerfully.[4]

According to income.

Every man shall give as he is able, according to the blessings of the LORD thy God which he hath given thee (Deuteronomy 16:17).

And all the tithe of the land, whether of the seed of the land, or of the fruit of the tree, is the LORD'S; it is holy unto the LORD (Leviticus 27:30).

Throughout the Old Testament, God's people gave the tithe (tenth) of their income to the Lord. Often, however, their giving far exceeded tithing. Tithing was the minimum. Some argue that this requirement was only for those of the Old Testament. They are merely arguing against a blessing. God's promise has never been rescinded.

According to ability.

And he looked up, and saw the rich men casting their gifts into the treasury. And he saw also a certain poor widow casting in thither two mites. And he said, Of a truth I say unto you, that this poor widow hath cast in more than they all: for all these have of their abundance cast in unto the offerings of God: but she of her penury hath cast in all the living that she had (Luke 21:1-4).

The poor widow's two mites, worth only a few cents at the most in today's coinage, did not enrich the Temple treasury by much. Her offering went unnoticed, except for Jesus' watchful eye. To Him it mattered, for she had exceeded her normal giving ability. It probably meant a forced fast. It went beyond her monthly budget.

Three things are outstanding about her giving. First, she was poor. "Penury" means great poverty; extreme want; destitution. Second, she gave all that she had, everything. Third, she was a widow. She had no husband to replenish her gift. Here is an example of genuine giving.

The tithe is a minimum requirement; when we give according to our ability above our tithe, we enter into an area of greater blessing. The promise and the command in Malachi include both tithes and offerings.

Without ostentation.

But when thou doest alms, let not thy left hand know what thy right hand doeth: that thine alms may be in secret: and thy Father which seeth in secret himself shall reward thee openly (Matthew 6:3-4).

A particular church member frequently managed to miss the offering plate only to walk down the aisle moments later with check in full view for all to see and to chase down an usher to give his gift. His testimonies typically went something like this: "I'm so thankful that God has blessed me. This week I was able to put an extra one hundred dollars in the offering." There is something distasteful about the manner in which he gave. He gave ostentatiously. Plainly put, he gave to impress others with his money.

Jesus taught us not to give so that others could see, and He further explained that anything done to impress people receives no reward from Him. In such a case, the giver's reward is the praise he receives from others; God owes him nothing.

We should not confuse secret giving with poor record keeping. Church records are kept confidential and therefore do not rob us of God's blessing. In fact the motive of someone who always gives anonymously (especially tithing) is questionable. For some, secrecy is a coverup for their lack of giving. Others give liberally but conscientiously object to anyone but God, including the IRS, knowing the extent of their gift. We should respect their conviction.

Give regularly.

Upon the first day of the week let every one of you lay by him in store, as God hath prospered him, that there be no gatherings when I come (I Corinthians 16:2).

All businesses have a financial budget, and the church does also. There are monthly expenses including utilities, insurance, mortgage payments, and missions, along with weekly responsibilities, typically salaries. Our giving should correspond to our flow of income and to the financial obligations of the church. The church should be able to count on us for weekly giving, or monthly if our income is monthly.

Though our tithe and basic offerings belong to our local assembly (God's storehouse), we must not overlook giving to various other needs such as a struggling widowed mother, ministries outside our local church, an unemployed neighbor, and so on. This giving of alms may include giving a five-dollar bill, donating a sack of groceries, or paying an electric bill for someone.

Standing with one hand open and extended heavenward and the other hand outstretched toward his class, Brother Wendell Gleason explained, "This is God's plan for giving. Keep one hand open to your fellow man and the other open to God. Let the blessings pass through you to others, and God will keep giving to you."

Give cheerfully.

Every man according as he purposeth in his heart, so let him give; not grudgingly, or of necessity: for God loveth a cheerful giver (II Corinthians 9:7).

To be a cheerful giver means to give joyfully, to be glad we can give, to be happy to give.

We must let go of our gift not only with our hand but with our heart also. The condition of the heart determines how God views the gift. As financially independent as God is, surely He despises receiving our money when our hearts are grumbling because we gave. But God loves it when we write out a check to the church while humming a beautiful hymn of praise.

God goes indebted to no one. This truth is beautifully illustrated by the account of the great catch of fish:

And it came to pass, that, as the people pressed upon him to hear the word of God, he stood by the lake of Gennesaret, and saw two ships standing by the lake: but the fishermen were gone out of them, and were washing their nets. And he entered into one of the ships, which was Simon's, and prayed him that he would thrust out a little from the land. And he sat down, and taught the people out of the ship. Now when he had left speaking, he said unto Simon, Launch out into the deep, and let down your nets for a draught. And Simon answering said unto him, Master, we have toiled all the night, and have taken nothing: nevertheless at thy word I will let down the net. And when they had this done, they inclosed a great multitude of fishes: and their net brake. And they beckoned unto their partners, which were in the other ship, that they should come and help them. And they came, and filled both the ships, so that they began to sink (Luke 5:1-7).

We can regard the catch of fish as payment for Jesus' use of Simon Peter's boat. Jesus borrowed the boat, and when He finished with it, He gave Peter a big tip for allowing Him to use it. There were two boats, for Peter had a business partner. Jesus used only one but He paid them both.

When we give to God, we can rest assured that He will bless us accordingly. Of course, our motive for giving must not be to get, and we must recognize that we can never buy, earn, or deserve God's blessings. But God will bless a faithful, obedient, and generous heart.

God's blessings are not always paid in dollars. The blessings for our cheerful giving come in varied forms. No dollar value can compare with love, joy, peace, health, happiness, and eternal life. We may be much richer than we realize.

Spend Wisely

Giving liberally to God's work does not offset our overspending. Someone said, "When our spending exceeds our income then our overhead becomes our downfall." This insight to spending is simple but extraordinary. The abuse of credit, coupled with high interest charges on goods that are not strictly necessary, causes many people to struggle financially. Too many identify with the typical American attitude of enjoy today and pay later. There is no overnight solution to this problem, but a night spent looking over bills and planning a long-range budget can eventually get a couple out of their debt dilemma. If after much consideration, they feel helpless financially, they should visit a reputable financial advisor as well as obtain spiritual counsel.

An excellent way to implement a long-range plan for paying off accumulated debts is to become consistent in

short-range goals. One advisor states, "Start with your
smallest bill and pay extra on it until it is paid in full. Then
go to the next smallest bill." There is wisdom in this
philosophy. The extra money paid on a small bill does not
hurt as much, and the debtor soon experiences the thrill
of seeing one bill completely wiped out. This success
motivates him to pay off another bill. And because he has
one less bill to pay, he has a little extra money to pay on
the next bill. One of the most exciting pieces of mail is
a mortgage note stamped "Paid in Full."

A practical financial formula suggested by George M.
Bowman is the 10-70-20 plan.[5] This financial formula is
also recommended by other Christian writers. Under this
plan, the money remaining after giving to the Lord and
the government is called "working money." This money
is to be divided into three areas: ten percent for savings
and investments, seventy percent for living expenses, and
twenty percent for debts and a buffer fund.

Another good piece of advice is to harness credit.
When someone is young and just starting out, it is difficult to obtain credit. But soon the situation reverses, and
credit becomes too easy to get. Many people overuse this
easy credit and pay an exorbitant interest rate as a result.
Monthly installments can shatter a budget. Consequently, credit must be kept within reasonable means. In
general, credit card purchases should be paid in full each
month to avoid steep interest rates, and installment purchases should be kept to a minimum. Credit purchases
equal to ten pecent of take home pay are usually reasonable. Some families may be able to manage fifteen percent, but twenty percent or more can cause a budget
deficit.

One couple has developed an interesting arrangement. The husband explains, "Some years ago my wife and I started something that we appreciate—separate checking accounts. Although both our names appear on both accounts, each of us is responsible for one. My paycheck is deposited into my account, which I use to pay bills such as housing, transportation, loans, insurance, and donations. I write my wife a check once a week for her checking account. She in turn purchases the groceries and other things as she chooses. There is a twofold purpose here. First, I establish a budget for our living expenses that she does not interfere with when she decides to buy a new dress. In turn, she is under no pressure from me regarding the money that she has. Since it is her checking account, however, she spends wisely, saving when possible for other things. Since she gets to enjoy the money she saves, she has the motivation to put a little more time and thought into her shopping. She has started using coupons and sometimes saves ten dollars a week on her grocery bill."

Every family needs a budget. For a family that is financially stable, budgeting may simply mean having a general idea of the flow of expenses during the month. For a family that is struggling financially, the budget should be detailed and closely monitored.

Once planned, a budget needs to be kept. The family can allow itself a reward for successful efforts. The reward may be anything from a special meal eaten out to a mini vacation—paid in cash instead of borrowed by credit card.

Save Consistently

A rule of thumb to remember about saving money is

"You can't save money spending it." We are all guilty of saying, "But it was such a good deal that I couldn't pass it up" or "I saved half the cost by buying today." We do not actually save when we spend money. We may be spending wisely, but we are not saving.

Americans are known for making more and saving less than people of other nationalities. Many Americans are very susceptible to advertisements. But let us consider this account of a family in South Korea. The husband made eight hundred dollars a month, which is quite good for that country, but of that amount his wife, who manages their money, saves five hundred dollars a month. They have purchased a house and are now saving for a car. They have learned to save.

Studies suggest that each generation is molded by prevailing conditions of its environment. For example, those who lived during the Depression era are more savings conscious. The conditions of the times prompted them to plan for the future. Others who have never experienced such an economic crisis may not see the need for saving. Their lack of foresight can prove to be a tragic error.

Saving and investing requires some expertise. It is wise to talk to a reputable professional on this subject, such as a banker, lawyer, or insurance representative. We must not fall prey to the get-rich-quick schemer who is here today and in jail tomorrow.

How much should we save? According to the 10-70-20 plan, after taxes and church giving, we should save ten percent of our income. It is wise to have both short-term and long-term savings. Short-term savings include money for Christmas expenses, a vacation, or furniture. Long-term savings include money for the down payment on a house, a new car, a college fund for the children, and retirement. An emergency fund is highly recommended.

An excellent article by Grace W. Weinstein, "Taking Charge of Your Finances," explains that a proper savings plan includes three elements: asset creation, asset accumulation, and asset protection.

Asset creation. Assets can be created by earning income and managing it well. The first step is to establish goals—what the family wants out of life financially (keeping the plan realistic). The second step is to make a budget and incorporate a savings plan within the budget. Anyone who is employed has the present means to save.

Asset accumulation. After a family implements a plan for the creation of assets it will begin to see an accumulation of assets. Much thought should be given to the types of savings desired: Long- and short-term savings, savings and checking accounts, certificates of deposit, money market funds, Individual Retirement Accounts (IRAs), mutual funds, stocks, bonds, pensions, real estate, and so on. Most of us have to start small with a savings account at a bank. But when this account reaches a reasonable amount, it should be placed into investments that bear greater interest.

Some say that all extra money should be placed in the work of the Lord. Certainly we should give sacrificially to God's work, but the Lord wants us to keep a balance. We should also prepare for the years when we can no longer work. We should not allow ourselves to become a burden to the church and others when we are retired. If we plan ahead now we can be a continued blessing to the church even after we have retired.

Some investments can be risky, such as common stock, undeveloped land, and corporate bonds. Other investments are rather safe, such as federally insured savings account, certificates of deposit (CDs), and a house. We should not place all our savings in risky investments, although they may offer the highest yields. It is wise to obtain reputable, qualified counsel in making investments.

Asset protection. A lifetime of savings can be wiped out by one unexpected illness. We can protect our assets in such a case by having proper health insurance. Life insurance protects the family in case of the death of the wage earner. And it is important to make a will prepared by an attorney to assure that the family receives the benefits we desire to leave them should we die, and with the minimum of red tape, expense, and potential conflict.

If possible, the wife should not work on a job outside the home while the children are young. Once they are in school, she may wish to obtain an outside job, seeking hours that harmonize with those of the school-age children. It is best to see them off to school and to be home when they return. If the second job is not strictly necessary, it should not be used for day-to-day living. The family should continue to live on the income of the husband, use the second income for savings and investment, and always remember that the wife's job may be terminated. For various reasons some families must depend on the income of working mothers. Their sacrifice does not go unnoticed by their children and peers, and God will reward them for their unselfish efforts.

Enjoy the Reward
Many people unnecessarily live with the constant fear

of financial disaster. They save and horde and live in dire poverty, rightly earning for themselves titles such as tightwad, miser, and Scrooge. An elderly widow wore the same simple dresses, day after day, denying herself even the necessities of life. She refused to throw away the tiniest thread while quilting feather ticks for mattressless beds. When she died, the children found a good sum of money that she had stored in fruit jars and hidden under the flooring of her house. She well knew how to save, but she never learned how to enjoy her reward. Her money proved to be useless to her, but needless to say, others enjoyed it very much.

Contrary to some Christians' theology, life is more than hard work and constant struggle. Paul wrote, "Charge them that are rich in this world, that they be not highminded, nor trust in uncertain riches, but in the living God, who giveth us richly all things to enjoy; that they do good, that they be rich in good works, ready to distribute [give], willing to communicate [share]" (I Timothy 6:17-18).

Clearly, some Christians in Paul's day were wealthy. They lacked for nothing financially. Paul admonished them to stay humble, not to put their trust in their wealth, to realize that money is only temporal, and to trust in God. He wanted them to recognize that all blessings come from God and to use their blessings to bless others. Verse 17 notes that God "giveth us richly all things to enjoy." Paul did not condone extravagance or ostentation, but neither did he deny enjoyment from the fruit of our labors.

Work hard! Give liberally! Spend wisely! Save consistently! But do not feel guilty for enjoying money. Take that needed vacation, or buy that new dress you have been admiring in the window for so long. But do not overlook the command to help and the joy of helping others— whether helping a needy family with groceries or sending some birthday cheer to a rest-home resident.

Someone said the only pathway to financial stability is, "Marry it, inherit it, or steal it." The saying is cute but not true. There are other means, notably through diligent work and the blessings of God. God wants us to prosper honestly. It does not normally happen overnight, but it is God's will for us.

Proposed Budget

Housing _____

Utilities _____

House upkeep _____

Food _____

Clothing _____

Transportation (vehicles, gas, upkeep) _____

Health Insurance _____

Life Insurance _____

Other Insurance _____

Income Taxes _____

Property Taxes _____

Installment purchases _____

Entertainment and recreation _____

Tithes _____

Contributions _____

Savings (10% after taxes and giving) _____

Other _____

_____

Monthly Expense _____

Total Monthly Income _____

Total Monthly Expense _____

Difference (plus or minus) _____

If expenses are greater than income, determine where to cut back. If income is greater than expenses, determine how to invest.

8

Meeting the Mortgage Payment:

The Mother Who Works outside the Home

*T*wo-thirds of American women work outside the home; many of them are mothers. Some work because they enjoy it, and others work to reach a desired goal, but most work because of financial demands: the mortgage payment comes due monthly. Whatever the reason, general problems confront the working mother.

From a biblical perspective, the ideal situation for a mother is to remain at home to care for small children, tend to the house, and greet children and husband with a kiss when they return. But the ideal is not always possible. And the ideal is sometimes misconstrued as a life of ease—fun and games raising the children.

On the contrary, the scriptural picture of the homemaker shows her diligent work:

Who can find a virtuous woman? for her price is far above rubies. The heart of her husband doth safely trust in her, so that he shall have no need of spoil. She will do

145

him good and not evil all the days of her life. She seeketh wool, and flax, and worketh willingly with her hands. She is like the merchants' ships; she bringeth her food from afar. She riseth also while it is yet night, and giveth meat to her household, and a portion to her maidens. She considereth a field, and buyeth it: with the fruit of her hands she planteth a vineyard. She girdeth her loins with strength, and strengtheneth her arms. She perceiveth that her merchandise is good: her candle goeth not out by night. She layeth her hands to the spindle, and her hands hold the distaff. She stretcheth out her hand to the poor; yea, she reacheth forth her hands to the needy. She is not afraid of the snow for the household: for all her household are clothed with scarlet. She maketh herself coverings of tapestry; her clothing is silk and purple. Her husband is known in the gates, when he sitteth among the elders of the land. She maketh fine linen, and selleth it; and delivereth girdles unto the merchant. Strength and honour are her clothing; and she shall rejoice in time to come. She openeth her mouth with wisdom; and in her tongue is the law of kindness. She looketh well to the ways of her household, and eateth not the bread of idleness. Her children arise up, and call her blessed; her husband also, and he praiseth her. Many daughters have done virtuously, but thou excellest them all. Favour is deceitful, and beauty is vain: but a woman that feareth the LORD, she shall be praised. Give her of the fruit of her hands; and let her own works praise her in the gates (Proverbs 31:10-31).

Many key phrases reveal the extent of the homemaker's hard work and her vital role. In this passage she

- Works willingly
- Rises early and stays up late
- Purchases land
- Gardens
- Ministers to the poor
- Sews for the family and also to make money
- Purchases food and cooks for the household
- Speaks with wisdom and kindness
- Is clothed with strength and honor
- Faithfully cares for husband and children
- Fears God

This passage certainly does not describe an idle wife who squanders away the hours protecting her smooth hands and filing her nails, waiting for a husband to get home from work to take her shopping.

Since necessity forces many mothers to work outside the home, the purpose of this chapter is not to create a guilt trip but to offer helpful suggestions. It is divided into two parts: Part I addresses the wife who works outside the home, while Part II addresses the husband of such a wife.

Part I
The Wife

Work describes life for the vast majority of women throughout history. The primary change has been only in the setting. In North America, beginning in the 1940s many women left the home and garden to work in an office or factory. Modernization has increased a woman's productivity. She tosses the laundry into the washer instead of using a scrub board, and the automatic dryer saves much time over the solar method of bygone years. The size of the family has decreased from ten to two. This is not to say she works any less, for she probably works about the same hours as her grandmother did. Rather, in many cases her work time is divided between the home and a work place away from home.

Some mothers who work outside the home blame their plight on husband or children. But blame and bitterness are not solutions. If the husband is working diligently but his income is not sufficient to meet the family lifestyle, a decision must be made. Either the family must alter its lifestyle to fit the husband's income, or else the wife must work a job outside the home. Particularly in the latter case, the wife must learn to overcome any bitterness. Her attitude toward the situation can be a blessing and example for her husband and children or a rancorous sore to the marriage and home. She can develop the proper attitude through prayer, Bible reading, and a positive outlook. She should accept the situation, see it as a challenge, and ask God to help her learn from it and be a light at her work place.

Beth decided that her job was her cross. She considered the crosses borne by Christian women of the early church—separation from families, cruel mistreatment, and martyrdom—and decided to bear her cross with dignity and love, without grumbling and complaining.

Insensitivity on the part of the husband can cause much frustration for the working mother. Many husbands view chores in the home and child care as women's work. Though it is only right that the husband share responsibilities in the home, especially when the wife must work outside the home, getting him to see this truth is often quite difficult. The problem is aggravated when the husband is unsaved and lives by a separate set of values. Men are also coerced by peers, who apply labels such as "hen pecked." Communication is the key to improving the sharing of responsibilities within the home.

Dealing with this issue is best done with a "TAP" and not a slap:
- Time
- Approach
- Place

The right timing is crucial. The wife should bring up the subject while the husband is in a good mood. The approach should be open, but not in an angry or attacking manner. The place should not be at a friend's house in an attempt to use friends for support.

More than likely, the problem will not be solved overnight. The husband may respond for a while but then lapse into his previous routines. It is important to keep communication lines open for future discussion, and normally it is best to keep parents out of this discussion.

Here is a sample approach: "George, may we talk a few minutes? I know that it's necessary for me to work a job outside the home. I love you and our family very much, and I want to do my part. Lately, because of the outside job, I'm running out of time, and I'm either not able to get all the work around the house done, or else, after I'm finished, I'm too tired to enjoy doing things with you and the children. I'm hoping there is some way we can rearrange the workload at home so I will have a little more time for the family. I've made up a work list to divide the responsibility at home among the entire family." This approach is neither demanding nor accusing.

149

From here the discussion could continue with input from the husband and children.

What should a working mother do when her husband is too insensitive to help even after she repeatedly asks? Many, feeling used and abused by a husband, look for a way out. Some escape into an extramarital affair. Some resort to excessive personal spending (a subtle way of getting even), others deny intimacy (another get-even tactic), and others seek divorce. Though revenge appeases one's anger for a while, and hysteria produces some effort on the part of the insensitive husband to help, these means do not promote a happy marriage but instead wreak an enormous emotional toll on the working mother.

At this point, it is advantageous to be firm but Christlike. Even if a husband refuses to change, refuses to seek counseling, refuses to read Part II of this chapter, or after reading it, refuses to accept it, the wife needs to remain Christ-like. She can determine to remain pleasing to her Lord and His Word.

And unto the married I command, yet not I, but the Lord, Let not the wife depart from her husband (I Corinthians 7:10).

Wives, submit yourselves unto your own husbands, as unto the Lord (Ephesians 5:22).

Likewise, ye wives, be in subjection to your own husbands; that, if any obey not the word, they also may without the word be won by the conversation [conduct] of the wives; while they behold your chaste conversation coupled with fear. Whose adorning let it not be that outward

150

adorning of plaiting the hair, and of wearing of gold, or of putting on of apparel; but let it be the hidden man of the heart, in that which is not corruptible, even the ornament of a meek and quiet spirit, which is in the sight of God of great price. For after this manner in the old time the holy women also, who trusted in God, adorned themselves, being in subjection unto their own husbands: even as Sara obeyed Abraham, calling him lord: whose daughters ye are, as long as ye do well, and are not afraid with any amazement (I Peter 3:1-6).

Wives, submit yourselves unto your own husbands, as it is fit in the Lord (Colossians 3:18).

Even if the husband acts like an enemy, Christ has commanded, "Love your enemies, bless them that curse you, do good to them that hate you, and pray for them which despitefully use you, and persecute you; that ye may be the children of your Father which is in heaven" (Matthew 5:44-45). Divorce does not cure everything; rather, in many cases, it produces problems equal to or greater than the predivorce situation. Christ promises to sustain us and wipe away all tears from our eyes (Revelation 21:4). Remaining Christian within a onesided marriage does not go unnoticed by the Lord.

These teachings do not mean that a wife should refuse to stand up for fairness in a marriage; rather, they are an encouragement for the wife to work diligently at keeping the family unit together.

Why are so many men insensitive to their wives in this area? A close examination reveals that most were socialized according to this pattern. Their mothers did all of the chores in the home, including washing all dishes, making all beds, and so on. Typically, the mothers and sisters took care of all the household chores, and the males worked hard all day to earn a living for the family. Mothers today who do not train their sons to help with household chores may help produce another generation that will reflect the same attitude as the present.

Another reason for insensitivity is that some men just do not enjoy cooking and cleaning. Women who detest changing the oil in the car or cleaning fish may relate to this feeling. Understanding the husband's makeup and selecting chores more suited to his nature would make the wife's efforts more successful.

Another problem confronts the working mother: she brings work pressure home. Discussing job stress with a spouse is helpful but should not be the conversation of the entire evening. The legal secretary must switch roles to be mother and wife at home.

Finding a babysitter is often a trying chore. Many struggle in deciding between a sitter's home versus a child-care center. Researchers now suggest that there is no major advantage to either. Though children who attend a center often score higher on IQ tests, the difference is quickly erased when children enter elementary school. Of primary concern should be whether or not the child is in an atmosphere compatible with one's Christian beliefs, and the type of physical care given. Questions to ask include: Who are the employees? What will be the activities of the day? How many other children will be there? What type of supervision is given? What kind of meals are served? What kind of discipline is administered? Is profanity allowed? What kind of music is played? (One day-care center played loud rock music daily.) It is also important to give consideration to the child's temperament. Some children adapt better to a smaller setting, while others are quite pleased to join in with larger groups. No research findings prove that there is one ideal for all children.

Finally, the working mother must establish priorities. Some things will not get done; others will not be done as efficiently as they could be if given more time. One working mother half jokingly said, "I look forward to the time when I can iron the whole shirts and not just the fronts." Twenty-four hours are all that are allotted to anyone, and battling against time may well produce frustration and fatigue. The wife must learn to allot so much time for each responsibility, including time for personal devotion and leisure. When supper is running late, and the husband and children demand, "We're starving!" the working mother can simply explain, "You can help speed it up by setting the table, or we can go out for pizza, or else everyone will just have to be patient." There is no need for anger or guilt.

Part II
The Husband

The era when only the husband worked outside the home is fading. In the majority of North American homes today, husbands and wives now share the responsibility of earning the family income. In short, the duties of the wife have been expanded, yet the husband's role remains about the same. Many men have readily adopted the new way for the wife (working outside the home), but they want to keep the old way for themselves, maintaining that housekeeping and child care are the woman's responsibilities. Yet one of the first things the army teaches a new recruit is to clean up his mess, make his bed, care for his clothes, peel potatoes, cook meals, and wash dishes. This work hurts the ego, but the increase of maturity is astounding.

Most men expect total freedom for themselves after eight hours on the job. Yet the wife who works eight hours in the office usually must come home to a routine evening packed full of cooking, cleaning, washing, folding, correcting, helping, caring, bearing, planning, canning, sewing, and perhaps anger—anger at a husband who is insensitive, selfish, and expects to be waited on by a "lucky" wife. One working mother expressed, "Why should women who have put in eight hours at the office or factory have to *ask* a husband for help?"

Many men feel that they are doing the wife a favor if they perform a chore, such as washing dishes or watching the children. They want pats on the back for an extra duty they perform, yet they express little, if any, appreciation to the wives who perform these duties daily. Husbands often ignore the mounting pressures on the wife until she blows her stack. One woman complained, "When my husband finally agrees to watch the children for an evening, he lets them run wild. When I return, the house is topsy turvy, the sink is full of dirty dishes, and I spend an hour or more cleaning up after them before I can retire to bed."

Church teachings have traditionally emphasized that the wife is the keeper of the house. Yet most women who work outside the home today do so at the request or desire of the husband. In light of this circumstance, we must reevaluate our philosophy. If a husband expects his wife

to work outside the home and then come home to perform most or all of the household chores, he is not fulfilling Scripture.

*Husbands, love your wives, even as Christ also loved
the church, and gave himself for it. . . . So ought men to
love their wives as their own bodies. He that loveth his wife
loveth himself. . . . Nevertheless let everyone of you in particular so love his wife even as himself, and the wife see
that she reverence her husband* (Ephesians 5:25, 28, 33).

For a man's life to exemplify these verses of Scripture, he must be sensitive to his working wife. If he expects her to work outside the home, then he must help
inside the home, for he is to show the same consideration to his wife as to himself. Otherwise, he is not express-
ing love for his wife, but rather selfishness and child-
ishness. Too many men want the wife to wait on them
like Mom did when they were young; they refuse to act
with maturity.

Where does a husband start when realizing his duty
to share responsibilities in the home? The husband and
the children can share numerous small tasks for which
the wife has been solely responsible. For example, the husband and children should be responsible for picking up
after themselves; dirty clothes should be put in a laundry basket, shoes arranged in the closet, and tools and
toys properly stored. Children should be taught to make
their own beds, and the husband, especially when he is
last to get up, should do the same. These tasks take but
a few minutes when shared but hours when done solely
by the mother/wife.

Cooking, normally reserved for the wife, can become a new adventure and challenge for the husband who occasionally makes his specialty. In this way he can offer the wife a welcome relief from the daily routine. After a meal, everyone should share in the cleanup. Doing dishes together can be a rewarding time of sharing, caring and communicating.

Since each home has its unique schedule, the husband (the head of the house), should call a family council to outline ideas for improving family relations. What an opportunity for Christian leadership in the home! For example, the family can list the duties that each person will be responsible for, such as cleaning up one's own room. Next, the family can list duties to be shared, classifying them by time and effort needed to accomplish them:

Group I	*Group II*	*Group III*
Dust the furniture	Carry laundry to basement	Wash the dog
Vacuum	Take out trash	Wash the car
Clean the bathroom	Water the flowers	Clean the patio

In a family of three, each person could choose one project from each group. Certain projects can be enjoyed as a family; raking leaves or washing windows can enhance family ties. Sharing the household responsibilities makes it possible for the wife/mother not only to have the time to enjoy family but also to have the energy to do so.

Some fathers of young children carry this concept of sharing to church also. Steve and Randy allow their wives to enjoy a service or participate more fully in worship by taking charge of the children during service from time to time.

Other couples take turns getting up at night with the baby for feeding or changing. One husband hired part-time cleaning help on Saturdays to free his wife for family activities on the weekend. Jeff arrives home before his wife does, so he prepares supper, and she does the dishes.

The husband is responsible for initiating this caring/sharing program. To wait for the wife to demand help is insensitive. The wife should not have to remind the husband that the grass needs to be mowed, the trash needs to be taken out, and the car needs to be washed.

Some men protest, "I doubt that Abraham ever did dishes." Neither did Sarah, or at least it is doubtful; she had a personal maid. If a wife works outside the home, then to preserve harmony within the home, not to mention the health of the working wife/mother, the husband and children must share in the chores of the home. The husband's marriage vows of devotion must extend beyond eight hours of work to provide income for the family, for the wife extended her eight hours of work in the home to include another eight hours in the work place to supplement the family income. It is not too late to start sharing responsibilities tonight.

House for Sale:

Single Parenting

Many families in North America, because of frequent moves, must feel they belong to the "Johnny Appleseed Society." Dreams of the nostalgic era when the children were raised at the old home place are fading. Most people do not see Grandma and Grandpa sitting in the evening on the front porch rocking. Someone confided, "Just how do you feel nostalgic about an apartment?" Families seldom live in the same house or neighborhood all of their lives. On the average, Americans move every three to five years. That statistic is mind boggling when we picture the stacks of boxes and mounds of crumpled newspaper packing necessary for each move.

No matter the reason for moving, one need always arises: the need for adjustment. The family who has moved must adjust to a new neighborhood, new grocery, new school, and new church. It seems there is no easy way or quick fix for these necessary adjustments.

These adjustments seem small, however, when we

compare them with the emotional adjustments that some families have to make due to death or divorce. The immediate result is a single-parent family. American statistics are shocking in this regard: one child in four lives with a single parent. This number is up from one in ten in 1960. Of those who live in a single-parent home, eighty-nine percent live with their mother.

This chapter could have been omitted thirty years ago, or at least skipped over by most readers. But today things are vastly different. In an article in *Focus on the Family*, Monica Dias and Sandy Kinser wrote:

> The American family is struggling to find its footing on a tightrope wobbling from the social upheaval of the past three decades. The fallout of the sexual revolution and women's movement made myth of the "nuclear family" of the 50's—the two-parent family with father as breadwinner and mother as homemaker. Only one in 10 families currently mirrors the stereotype, according to the Work and Family Information Center of the Conference Board in New York.
>
> The sexual revolution brought open marriage, no-fault divorce and alternative lifestyles. The women's movement brought working mothers and changes in child-rearing roles and child-care responsibilities.
>
> Collectively, the movements created more two-career families, single-parent families and remarriages with different combinations of stepparents and stepchildren.[1]

All of us know of a single-parent family. Yet many

of us, because of the commonness of the situation, seem insensitive to the fears, frustrations, and needs of the single-parent family.

Both the single parent and the children have difficulties, and both need to be addressed. For example, the responsibilities of the single parent are doubled. Whereas many of the problems of the traditional home can be solved simply by purchasing a second car, this is not so with the single parent. Many mothers must do the normal homemaker chores, be the breadwinner, try to be a father to the children (toss ball, take them fishing, go on picnics, and so on), do all the correcting, be their spiritual leader, take them to school, help with the homework, keep the house repaired, mow the lawn, find a reputable mechanic, and the list goes on and on and on. Her job is doubled, and her pressures are multiplied. The same is true for the single father. As an example, a single father enrolled his six-year-old in a Christian school. The father left for work at seven AM and did not return until six PM. School began at nine AM and dismissed at three PM. He faced many difficulties with sitters and transportation, but he had no one else to lean on.

One of the greatest responsibilities of the single parent is facing decisions alone. The burden of win or lose rests solely upon one set of shoulders. There is no one to caution, "I don't think it will work," or to encourage, "Go for it!" And the blame cannot be shared. It is either his fault or her fault, but never their fault.

The single parent goes to the adult Christmas banquet, adult Sunday school class, or church picnic alone. The loneliness can be a constant companion and reminder of a loss, a divorce, a heartbreak, a mistake, or a failure.

161

The Christian single parent may struggle spiritually with bitterness or anger toward the husband or wife who is not there, and may also struggle with normal physical desires that no longer have a permissible release. Peace and joy may be replaced with guilt and frustration.

The children of a single parent are faced with their own set of problems. The void caused by a lack of a male or female image in their life may lead to emotional difficulties for the child. The child is often embarrassed by the questions that the single-parent situation produces: "Who is your father? Why doesn't your dad live with you?" In an attempt to avoid embarrassing questions, the child may withdraw socially or be overly defensive. He may feel insecure, slighted, or angry. Children, especially ages six to twelve, may experience a false sense of guilt. Some assume that they lost their parent because they weren't good enough for the missing parent to accept. They may also fear that the parent they now have will also leave them. They tend to hang on to the hope of a reconciliation between divorced parents, and sometimes try to cause it to happen. These children often suffer academically.

Because the single parent must work outside the home, the children will have to spend much time with a sitter or in a day-care facility. While many children adapt very well, others struggle. They learn to hate divorce, and often the parent whom they feel caused the divorce. Usually they blame the one who walks out even though he or she may not be primarily responsible. Robert Taylor stated, "Children really never understand divorce. They learn of it, accept it, and make necessary adjustments. But they never understand."[2]

Some children are forced to grow up with an unwanted, unwarranted, unfair title attached to their names: illegitimate. Such a label makes them bear the guilt of the parents' error. The young child may often blame self for not having a father or mother. As a result, emotional imbalances linger even into adulthood. The question "Why?" is ever on their lips. "Why didn't my dad send me a birthday present?" One small lad, after such an occasion, angrily told his mother, "I don't like my dad anymore. Why don't you get me another dad?"

This anger is normal, and children need to express it. One psychologist suggested that it is similar to putting air in a balloon. If some air is not released but air continues to be added, the balloon will eventually burst. Frustration due to the neglect of an absent parent needs to be discussed without allowing the child to have fits of anger, throw objects, or slam doors. The single parent will have to help the child deal with the anger in a constructive manner. Unless the child is allowed to express his feelings, the adult may not know what the child is experiencing inside.

Jane grew up without the love of a father. At age fifteen she was hanging onto any male who would show her attention. Many mistook her excessive show of affection as promiscuous desire, but she was only seeking the father image that she did not have.

Jim lost his mother at a young age. He would call a girlfriend's mother "Mom" at first meeting. The girl's mother considered this too forward and assuming, but he was merely in quest of a mother's love that he had missed as a child. These two people have carried their emotional losses into adulthood.

Financial problems often plague the single-parent family. The expense of child care is consuming, but most single mothers cannot quit their jobs and care for the children as they desire. Child support from an absent father is often slow and erratic or sometimes nonexistent. The mother may have to choose between accepting child support and thereby allowing visitation rights to a non-Christian father who is a tragic influence on the child, or trying to make it alone without financial support. Single-parent fathers also struggle financially. These are but a few of the many concerns facing the single-parent home.

Many churches have no programs that minister to the single-parent home. Counsel and physical help are not always available for their needs. But this situation can be improved. We must not overlook the single parents or their children. A Friday evening family cookout could include a single-parent family. With a little extra effort we can give attention to a child who may be questioning his self-worth. A birthday card or gift would brighten his day. He can become our responsibility on the next father-son outing. A childless couple could select a single-parent family and share their love with them. We can offer a listening ear and heart to the bewildered single mother. We can encourage her, take her to the next ladies auxiliary meeting, or offer to babysit for her during some special occasion. May all of us do our best to fulfill the emotional, spiritual, and material needs in the single-parent family.

Though the single-parent family is not the ideal situation, it is far from impossible. Robert Taylor said, "The one-parent family is often a spectacular success."[3] It is often better than living in a home characterized by constant yelling, fighting, and mental or physical abuse. The Bible describes how undesirable husband-wife conflict is: "It is better to dwell in a corner of the housetop, than with a brawling woman in a wide house" (Proverbs 21:9). Brawling refers to constant quarreling in a noisy, disorderly, and sometimes physically abusive manner. Studies suggest that some families who are forced to live with a single parent are better off alone than if they lived in constant turmoil.

Many have no choice in the matter. In either situation, a person must make the best of it. Perhaps the situation is the result of a tragic mistake, for which the person must now bear the consequences. In this case Christ will forgive, and His strength and guidance will be available as the person accepts his or her responsibilities. Or the situation may result from the misfortune of a mate's premature death, in which case God's grace can comfort and sustain.

Here are some suggestions to help the single parent not only survive the battle but come out a radiant Christian.

Offset loneliness by involvement with people. In addition to the ministries of the local church, there are numerous charitable service organizations with which the single parent can choose to become involved. Volunteering at a local hospital is an excellent example. While helping others, the single parent can also enjoy much needed fellowship. Involvement combats loneliness. Loneliness can be dealt with—perhaps not completely abolished, but controlled.

The single parent should not allow holidays to catch

him or her without plans. It may require some initiative to ensure fellowship on these occasions.

The single parent must allow Jesus Christ to be a close friend and should nurture daily fellowship with Him. Christian music in the home can dispel gloominess, take the mind off the day-to-day rat race, and help focus attention on the positive.

Retain family ties. After one man divorced his lovely Christian wife, leaving her with a small child, the in-laws realized that the divorce was not their daughter-in-law's doing. They had fallen in love with her and their grandchild. After the divorce they still treated her as their own. Their love has been a comfort and great help to the daughter-in-law, and the grandchild has a loving relationship with his grandparents. Not all are blessed to have such wonderful in-laws, but the single parent should attempt to cultivate family relationships without being intrusive.

As much as possible, the single parent should remain close to the family and avoid isolation. The children need the love of both paternal and maternal grandparents, uncles, aunts, cousins, and so on. They need to realize that they belong to a big family who loves them.

Develop friendships. It is best to have a close friend in whom to confide deepest fears, frustrations, disappointments, and joys. But it does not need to be a one-way relationship. The friend may also need friendship, ears to listen, and a shoulder to cry on. The single parent's experiences can help him or her to become empathetic of the needs of others.

But avoid rushing friendships; they need time to grow. Do not cling to people, but give friends room. Even a close friend may not want to see or hear from you every day.

Avoid the appearance of evil, and avoid fornication.
Single parents may find it more difficult to control passions than the person who has never been married, due to past experiences within the bounds of marriage. Even though they have reached a mature age, their dates still need to be well planned, and they should avoid spending prolonged time together at home alone with a date. "But I'm mature!" some argue. Nevertheless, they are also human and vulnerable to passions that may be aroused in an opportune environment. Discretion may also keep tongues from wagging.

Someone can date for fellowship without giving the impression to every date that he or she is pining for marriage. If a person does not take matters slowly, he or she could prevent a lasting relationship from developing.

Become acquainted with helpful organizations. There are various governmentally sponsored programs designed to aid the single-parent home. A single parent in need should not deprive self or children of these resources because of pride. A Christian can also accept charity graciously without losing a feeling of independence or self-worth. Many communities offer free counselling for the single-parent family. But the Christian must guard against humanistic counselors that offer unbiblical advice.

Get involved at church. The single parent may feel awkward at first, since most of the adults are married, but church involvement is vitally important. The children need to be involved with rallies, summer camp, and the various church activities. Involvement will mean extra work, but it is well worth the effort. Getting the children to youth activities at the local church and promoting Christian fellowship for them are essential. For example, a teenage boy should be allowed to have the church guys over for pizza and games sometimes. The single parent can even become a parent helper for the youth group.

Instead of waiting to be asked, the single parent should volunteer for hospital or shut-in visitation, or help with the props for the Christmas play, or look for ways to be a blessing to the local church. And of course, faithfulness in church attendance is extremely important.

Make communication in the home a daily habit. The single parent, trying to make a living for the kids, may come home mentally and physically exhausted. A short time of relaxation alone can help him or her feel more like talking and sharing with the family. It is much better to vacuum once a week and have time to talk and play with the kids than to vacuum daily and be irritable and withdrawn. Chores can be shared, allowing everyone to have quality time together afterwards.

Take time to listen. Do not force communication but give ample opportunity for it. Answer all questions, especially the ones parents prefer avoiding. Children need reasons for the single-parent status. But these answers should not prevent them from loving the absent parent. Their burden is heavy enough without heaping onto their shoulders your emotions. Consider this true example.

Jeff felt neglected by his father, who had remarried. He was limited to a small amount of time with his dad. This feeling could have been magnified into hate for the father with a little coaching from his mother. Being young, he did not understand all the reasons for the divorce. When he graduated from college a few years ago, he discussed his feelings of rejection. "Things are much better now," he said. "I visit more with my father. I even understand why he gave me so little time growing up. It was actually his wife's fault. She felt threatened every time he saw me. Therefore, she fought his being with me." What if Jim's mother had instilled hate by such comments as, "Your father doesn't love you. He never visits you and doesn't want you visiting him"? Jeff may have suffered deeper emotional problems, and he and his father may never have developed the relationship they now enjoy.

The children should be taught respect for the absent parent if possible. This teaching helps ensure respect for a stepparent as well. The single parent should not force the children into a situation where they must take sides emotionally. If there are difficulties with the other parent, an attempt should be made to work them out without involving the child. Of course, the single parent must not lie or be dishonest with the children, but when questions are asked, choice words can soften the harsh impact on the children.

To make up for the children's missing parent, the single parent may be tempted to spoil them by giving in to outlandish wishes, demands, and even rebellion. One single mother felt obligated to buy her child a gift each time she went shopping. The child's response was not gratitude but greater demands. A parent must not allow or instill a "poor me" attitude, or it may follow the child all through life. Some adults feel that the world owes them something extra because they did not have a father or a mother. They would be much more productive had they been taught to accept their loss and make the best of it.

Think twice before marriage. Study the scriptural teaching regarding your options, and think through

169

motives for remarriage. These motives can vary from seeking a father or mother for the children to seeking someone to be the breadwinner or housekeeper. But a new marriage needs the solidity and strength of love to last; other motives should be side benefits or else secondary.

Forcing children to accept a new father or mother often dashes their hopes of a reconciliation between their real parents. Patience is a virtue here. The child may need time to learn to love a stepparent.

One single father married to offer his children a replacement for their loving mother, who had recently died. His new bride had other motives in mind, including financial security. She was not ready to mother three new children plus her own daughter. Frustrations mounted in the home, and mental abuse of the children was the outcome. The older son left home as soon as possible. He remains bitter toward his stepmother, father, church, and God. The younger son survived by developing a close association with his church family, but emotional scars remain. The third child, a little girl, is totally confused. She is torn between her love for her stepmother, the only mother she remembers, and her love for her brothers, who resent the stepmother. To complicate matters further, when the family finances were exhausted because of exorbitant spending, the stepmother ended the marriage with divorce.

Honesty and caution should accompany any new relationship. The single parent should pray much before making any commitments for marriage and should discuss these feelings and plans with the pastor.

Give Christ time in your life. Though the single parent has a double workload, he or she has available the time that would normally be spent with a spouse. This time can be dedicated to Christ. Paul wrote to the singles in the church at Corinth:

But I would have you without carefulness. He that is unmarried careth for the things that belong to the Lord, how he may please the Lord: but he that is married careth for the things that are of the world, how he may please his wife. There is difference also between a wife and a virgin. The unmarried woman careth for the things of the Lord, that she may be holy both in body and in spirit: but she that is married careth for the things of the world, how she may please her husband (I Corinthians 7:32-34).

A single status enables someone to be a special blessing in God's kingdom. Such was the prophetess Anna. At a very young age her husband had died. She chose to remain unmarried, becoming a worker in the Temple:

And there was one, Anna, a prophetess, the daughter of Phanuel, of the tribe of Aser: she was of a great age, and had lived with an husband seven years from her virginity; and she was a widow of about fourscore and four years, which departed not from the temple, but served God with fastings and prayers night and day (Luke 2:36-38).

Her devoted life to God gave her the insight that Jesus was the Christ years before most people understood who He was. She was able to hold the Christ child in her arms, understanding that He was Israel's Messiah. Devotion to Christ gives the single person the opportunity for unique ministries.

171

Seek contentment rather than change. New surroundings are not always the best. A new spouse is not a guarantee of happiness. Christians should seek for contentment in their present state rather than seeking contentment through change of status. This teaching does not suggest passiveness or a lack of effort to better oneself, but it is intended as a caution and reminder that to seek happiness in things is not good. Rather, one should seek contentment in God. Paul wrote, "Not that I speak in respect of want: for I have learned, in whatsoever state I am, therewith to be content" (Philippians 4:11). To be at peace with self in an unpleasant situation can assure happiness whether or not life's changes bring blessings.

A chapter alone cannot address all the needs, frustrations, and challenges of the single-parent home. But perhaps this chapter can help the church to become more aware of the single-parent family and can offer some direction for the single parent. Though the single-parent family is certainly not the ideal situation, the goal of the single parent can and should be more than survival. Each situation, though it may share similarities with others, is looked upon and cared for by Jesus Christ on an individual basis. Although there are 8,600 species of birds and millions of individual birds of each species, He notices each sparrow that falls. How much more does He care for human concerns! Let us cast our cares upon Him, for He has asked us to do so (I Peter 5:7). He truly cares about all our needs, fears, and frustrations.

10

Stepparents and Stepchildren

T he stepparent must fulfill what is often a very awkward and pressure-filled role. One can be a hero or a goat.
With the setting already established, the stepparent must
assume a leading role without a rehearsal with the cast.
Likewise, the stepchild finds himself in a totally unfamiliar
and often undesired situation. Making the adjustment is
seldom easy and often very difficult, but a host of families
can testify to a very positive outcome.

Let us explore the role of a stepparent in three situations: death, divorce, and dual stepparents. Each must
be looked at through the eyes of the stepparent and the
stepchild.

Stepparents Created by Death

A stepparent arrangement created by the death of
a spouse followed by remarriage can result in one of two
extremes. The stepchild may readily accept the stepparent
to fulfill the emptiness created by the loss of a parent,

or the stepchild may cling to memories of the deceased parent. The child may resent anyone who tries to take the place of a former parent. If this is the case, the stepparent must find or create ways to assure the child that he or she is not trying to take the place of the deceased parent but merely trying to pick up where the biological parent was forced to stop. Here are some suggestions to help children cope with such resentment.

1. Allow children to talk about the deceased parent. Encourage, but do not force them to talk.

2. Do not try to force them to accept. They may confuse acceptance with having to stop loving the deceased parent, which can easily cause guilt on the part of an already confused child. Sometimes the child feels personally responsible for the death; this is especially true among children ages six to twelve.

3. To defuse resentment, encourage, but do not force, the child to keep a picture of the deceased parent in his or her room. This is an open expression of nonaggression on the part of a stepparent.

4. Allow plenty of time for the child to accept love from the stepparent. The stepchild needs time to let go of the past. Children under nine years of age do not understand death, and so they may cling to the past, waiting for the deceased parent to return.

5. Do not become intimidated by a deceased parent. Acknowledge a feeling of intimidation as a subtle form of jealousy and deal with it both intellectually and spiritually to remove it.

6. When children finally come around with acceptance, do not hold past actions against them.

The child may experience doubts about God's love,

asking questions like, "Why did God take my parent?" This is a normal behavioral pattern. Do not become overly alarmed. Offer an explanation and assurance of God's love.

Wanting to be accepted, the stepparent sometimes goes overboard, trying to compete with the former parent. This can only present frustration. The stepparent cannot play such an assumed role indefinitely. On the other hand, the stepparent can use this opportunity to make improvements in his or her life.

One problem area that typically needs better handling is the time leading up to the remarriage. Too often the stepchild is introduced to the stepparent a day or so before the wedding. Meeting the children much earlier can eliminate shock or at least give the children some time to absorb the change before they are living in the same house with a stepparent. Many children would probably have responded differently to a marriage if they had been included in the arrangements. Perhaps a child can be included in the wedding party, but again, only if the child wants to.

Much discussion should take place before the marriage. The couple should consider the following questions, along with others, and reach a mutual agreement on these matters.

1. Who will discipline the children and how?

2. What type of responsibilities are expected of the children from both parents?

3. Suppose the child is a teenager. What type of curfew is expected?

4. What are the telephone, car, and visiting privileges?

5. How much allowance does the child receive, and who provides it?

Stepparenting creates a tremendous need for communication between the spouses and the child. The arrangement causes a great deal of readjusting. The husband and wife must adjust to each other, but at the same time, one of them must adjust to a child or children and the children must adjust to a stepparent. The children often struggle with resentment of their parent for accepting another mate other than their own biological parent. The situation created is indeed delicate. Many counselors suggest that the family conduct a weekly share time when everyone can discuss likes, dislikes, complaints, hurts, and so on. This time can be a tremendous opportunity for growth. The family should always include prayer in this time of communication.

Another adjustment is for the stepchildren to be introduced to their new stepgrandparents. That gives them six grandparents. Though not as traumatic, this adjustment can be stressful on the child, especially if this relationship is forced. Sometimes the stepgrandparents are resentful. To prevent any unnecessary stress on the child, this relationship should be allowed to develop over a period of time. Depending upon the circumstances, the relationship may never develop beyond an acquaintance. The parents should not be overly concerned if this is the case. It is acceptable and will not harm the child emotionally.

Stepparents Created by Divorce

This chapter is not intended to establish scriptural teachings on divorce and remarriage, but simply to address the needs in this area of stepparenting. Questions regarding divorce and remarriage should be discussed with a pastor. Regardless of past rights or wrongs in a situation, our purpose is to offer help for families now in this situation.

The adjustments caused by divorce and remarriage can be very difficult for both the stepparent and the stepchild. Though the stepchildren may accept the stepparent, they still have another parent alive, who may come and go in their lives. Such a transition often creates a very traumatic adjustment—sometimes every week. At a seminar on "Helping Children Cope with Divorce," a schoolteacher stated, "You can always tell on Monday if the child has visited with the other parent on the weekend." Different emotions are displayed—anywhere from misbehavior to withdrawal. The stepparent and biological parent should realize that a child needs time to readjust when he or she returns home from visiting the other biological parent. The weekend parent can sometimes overdo gifts, privileges, and so on. Parents should not become overly alarmed if the child withdraws to his or her room for the first few hours back home. Nor should parents feel that the child is being disrespectful. If the child returns home boisterous, it is not necessarily a sign of disrespect or rebellion. It may be that this behavior has been the normal weekend pattern. Though law and order and reality may have to be restored, it should be done with understanding.

Nina Begley, a staff therapist for a family consulting center, stated:

> When divorce occurs, children experience many different feelings. Anger at one or both parents is fre-

quent, with a strong focus on the one who initiated the divorce. Children often feel responsible for the parents' divorce. They feel the guilt of thinking that they must have done something wrong to cause the divorce.

Coupled with the anger and guilt are fears of abandonment and embarrassment. The children often think they have been deserted by one parent and fear that the custodial parent will leave them as well. They also struggle with the same embarrassments adults face: "What will family and friends think and how do I tell them?"

Hope of reconciliation is common among children who are struggling to cope with divorce. This hope may persist until one or both parents remarry and even afterwards.

It is evident that children have no built-in automatic adjustment system. The road to adjustment is a long, winding path with uncertainties lingering beyond each curve. Success as a stepparent depends a great deal on understanding and patience.

A stepparent must accept the fact that there has been another person in his or her spouse's life. Since the stepchild is a constant reminder of this fact, the stepparent must make sure that he or she does not show resentment to the child either openly or subtly, deliberately or unconsciously. The stepparent should pray for the ability to accept the child as his or her own.

Dual Stepparents
One of the common problems of dual stepparenting

is a question of fairness. "You treat your child better than you treat mine" is an oft spoken complaint. The principles of communication discussed in chapter 2 can help alleviate or resolve this problem. Since discussions and arguments in this area often end in deadlock, it may be necessary to seek counsel from a pastor or another professional. Usually, all involved will have to bend a great deal. The unbiased counselor can assure fairness in this area.

Bringing two families together can create a sensitive situation. One potential problem is the possibility of physical attraction between a teenage stepbrother and stepsister. This situation calls for understanding and family communication.

A delicate situation often results when one family moves in with the other. The moving family may feel like and be treated as an intruder, since the house belongs to the "other family." An oft spoken complaint is "This is my room. I don't want to share it." Some family counselors suggest that the blended family move into a new house if possible. In this way, everyone starts on an even basis with no one being intruders.

Though the insights of a qualified counselor are not always what we want to hear, we should accept such insights as usually being clearer than our own. As an example, one stepmother complained that her stepson was too loud. Her conclusion, however, was drawn from a comparison of the stepson with her biological son. What she did not consider was that her son was abnormally shy and withdrawn. It took an unbiased counselor to help her see this truth. She probably would not have accepted the same observation from her husband. As a result, she was able not only to accept her stepson, but also to help her own son with his problems.

Stepparenting is a noble act. All children belong to Jesus Christ, and His smile is upon those who extend love and help to children who are not their own biologically, and seek to raise them as their own. After all, it is He who said, "Suffer little children, and forbid them not, to come unto me: for of such is the kingdom of heaven" (Matthew 19:14).

11

Home Insurance

Protection through Midlife

*W*e seldom hear of an uninsured house, for the gamble is too risky. We do not take a chance that our house will never be the victim of fire, vandals, or the elements. We pay premiums without fail, often for years, without ever having to use our insurance.

Then it happens. The wife forgets a roast in the oven while she stretches her Christmas shopping. Five hours later, charge cards exhausted, she returns home to a smoke-filled house. When she phones her husband to break the news, the first question is, "Did we make the insurance payment?"

The problem is seldom a lack of insurance, but sometimes there is a problem of being underinsured. Too many discover this after the damage has occurred.

Let us consider marriage in light of this analogy. Each stage of marriage brings areas of vulnerability that require extra protection. One such stage is midlife. No one reaches sixty without going through ages thirty-five to

181

fifty-five. As these years usher in signs of aging, many people panic and grab for straws of reassurance.

Many men reject the idea that they will experience such nonsense. But a whopping eighty percent will. One wife confided, "The tapes I purchased on midlife described my husband to a T, but he won't listen to them! How do you help someone like that?"

First, we must understand that no one is exempt. We all must grow older. Second, we must understand that a normal process of aging takes place. Though midlife varies with individuals, it is usually defined as between thirty-five and fifty-five years of age. Physically the body changes; it is half worn out. The battle of the bulge rages, brought on by slowed metabolism. Athletic abilities wane. A teenage son can outrun his middle-aged father. Gray hair and wrinkles frighten most of us.

The anxiety level often reaches a peak during midlife. Job burnout causes the male to contemplate getting away from the hustle and bustle of the daily work routine. He may even consider a career change. He often feels that he has climbed as high as he can go on the job, yet he fears that the younger college graduates are only one rung below him. He is a letter away from resigning without understanding why. One man struggling through midlife expressed, "I feel like taking a leave of absence for a year or so and doing some traveling up north. I've always wanted to visit Alaska." Only reality and loyalty restrains the man in this situation. He cannot quit his job. He is trapped by responsibilities: braces for Junior, college tuition for Susie, and ten more years of house payments. Unaccomplished goals dangling in front of his face defy his grasp. The clock is ticking. Failures hover as if trying to find a landing pad in the back yard. Retirement is around the corner, but financial preparations are still incomplete.

Many men become concerned about virility. Fears sometime lead to experimentation; experimentation leads to infidelity.

As with men, women are not all affected in the same manner by midlife. One lady said she never knew when midlife began or ended. She is fortunate. For other women midlife can be a traumatic experience. During menopause, the hormone level falls, setting off a period of emotional ups and downs. One woman overreacted to small happenings in the household with crying jags, and she fought sporadic bouts of depression. Hot flashes and sleeplessness often aggravate the situation.

Every person who nears this stage needs to be aware of the symptoms of midlife crisis. A thorough understanding of the changes that take place chemically and physically will help a person to remain in control of emotions. The person can say, "I feel depressed today. But I realize it is due to changes within me and not a result of outside circumstances. I will take charge of my emotions and focus my attention on chores that need to be completed, or set some new goals for my life." A person can refuse to be a slave to emotions.

This chapter is only an introduction. Religious bookstores carry thorough reading material on the middle years. No one should tackle midlife as an illiterate.

The following pages present some suggestions for weathering the storms of the middle years.

Understanding

Not everyone experiences the same degree of physical or emotional changes. A spouse may have more difficulty than the mate. No one has all the answers, but each one can understand what is creating the problems. Spouses should not take thoughtless remarks so personally. An argument is not the solution, but understanding often is. The couple should concentrate on ways to combat the emotional battles instead of battling one another.

Assurance

Psychological warfare often rages during midlife. Self-esteem is on the line. The person in midlife crisis typically wonders, Am I a lesser person? Do I still fulfill the needs of my wife (or my husband)? Am I attractive? For example, Kay thought the worst if her husband was a few minutes late getting home from work.

In this situation, the positive assurance of a spouse is soothing balm. This assurance must be spoken and shown. "Yes, we are growing older, but our love is growing deeper. Our love is more than youthful infatuation. We love in spite of faults. Gray hair was never more beautiful. The wrinkles around your eyes remind me of the years of laughter we have shared. Through triumph and sorrow, sickness and health, good times and bad, we have never stopped loving. We face a new challenge. We will be here for each other because we understand. Yesterday I couldn't cope, and you held me up. Tomorrow you may need my help. Hand in hand, we grow older and closer."

In offering assurance, "a word fitly spoken is like apples of gold in pictures of silver" (Proverbs 25:11). A husband should not say, "I love you even though you aren't as attractive as you used to be." Instead, "You are lovely to me." The wife shouldn't comment, "I think you are still handsome even though you are bald now." She should stop with the compliment and forget the comparison.

Guarding Fidelity

Some couples, for various reasons, experience sexual problems during the middle years. Too often some are tempted to experiment, to prove mostly to themselves that they are not has-beens. For some men, it is a time when younger women look up to them. The younger woman may see the older male as matured, successful, and having arrived. He misinterprets her friendliness as being suggestive. She acknowledges his invitation to lunch as a business compliment, or perhaps as a step toward a promotion. He experiences an ego high. The drama often ends tragically.

The Scriptures warn of those who are adulterers at heart. "For the lips of a strange woman drop as an honeycomb, and her mouth is smoother than oil: but her end is bitter as wormwood, sharp as a twoedged sword. Her feet go down to death; her steps take hold on hell" (Proverbs 5:3-5). The adulterer's list of conquests includes boss, neighbor, secretary, and repairman. The person in midlife must not be so foolish. "Remove thy way far from her [the harlot], and come not nigh the door of her house: lest thou give thine honour unto others, and thy years unto the cruel" (Proverbs 5:8-9). The Scriptures admonish us to guard against situations that tempt to infidelity.

Couples should censor their reading material. Some

married women drool over romance stories like lovesick teenagers. Some men select questionable literature from magazine racks. Someone said it well, "What the eye reads, the mind perceives, and the heart too often believes." Fantasizing about someone else as a sexual partner is not only harmful, it is sin.

During midlife, many factors can take a toll on romance. Both marriage partners begin to slow down physically. Fascination has become familiarity. Routine has replaced the mystery. Responsibilities and job-related stress are hard to drop outside the bedroom door.

To help keep romance alive, many mini-vacations work wonders. The change of scenery, absence of children, and relief from jangling phones have a rejuvenating effect. No one expects forty-five-year-olds to constantly behave like newlyweds, but an annual honeymoon is marvelous medicine for midlife.

One couple realized their bedroom had become the location for discussions regarding frustrations at home and at work. The discussions were healthy, but they were much more beneficial when held somewhere else. The couple further corrected their bedroom blahs by retiring before exhaustion. Other helpful factors are fresh sheets, personal cleanliness, and a pleasant, loving attitude. Someone said, "Sex is ninety percent mental." Certainly, a person's attitude about self and mate greatly enhances or harms a physical relationship.

II Samuel 11 records the mistakes of a Bible favorite, King David. When we read about his heroic deeds, his humility, his loyalty to Saul, his faith in the Lord, and his worship, we are inspired by this tremendously godly man. But then the depth of his sin unfolds. We would like to erase it and pretend it never happened. But it did. King David not only committed adultery, he tried to hide his crime by eliminating a potential accuser, his loyal warrior, Uriah.

King David was approximately forty-five years old when he plunged head first into the pitfalls of infidelity. Yes, he was in the midlife years. When other kings went forth to battle, King David stayed home. Why? At forty-five, there was still plenty of fight in him. He was far from a has-been warrior. Yet the sound of battle, the clashing of iron against iron, the strategy of war, and the thrill of victory all seemed to have lost their motivation for King David. The bear-killing, giant-slaying hero of Israel waved goodbye as Joab and the Lord's army marched out to battle.

Perhaps the scenario went something like this. David was in emotional turmoil. Unspoken thoughts troubled him. At late evening, sleep evading him, he arose from bed and walked upon the roof terrace of his palace. "Am I too old? Does Israel still need me, or am I a worn-out sandal? Do my valiant men respect me as their warrior king, or do they serve me out of obligation? Do my wives find me romantic or boring?" The full moon lit the courtyard and the adjoining dwellings. Jerusalem was preparing for bed. David's wandering thoughts were suddenly interrupted. What a beautiful woman and youthful! How would she feel about dining with me, the king of all Israel? "Servant, who is that woman? Find out for me."

The following day, inquiry disclosed that she was married to one of David's own mighty men, the youthful Uriah. This failed to deter a dinner invitation from the king to Bathsheba. Presumably, a zest for life returned to the palace. Goliath's challenge, echoing across the Judean valley, was born afresh in King David as he rehearsed his dinner conversation. Donning his most royal garments he prepared for what proved to be the biggest battle he ever lost: midlife. Neither before nor after would King David commit such sin. It came during the middle years.

An analysis of the king's behavior during midlife reveals a harshness in David's behavior that did not seem to be present in his earlier years. When the prophet Nathan came to rebuke David's sin, he told a parable about a rich man who stole a pet lamb from a poor man in order to feed a traveler. We can agree that the selfish rich man in Nathan's story should have been punished— perhaps a year at public service, or restitution of a hundredfold, or an embarrasing public hearing. But David, not realizing the story was a parable, demanded death! Death seems to be a ridiculously harsh verdict. But it is typical of the irrational behavior of a person in midlife who is troubled within; who is void of assurance from associates, family, and friends; and who refuses to accept midlife graciously.

Some people in midlife crisis may feel that it is too late for them to overcome. Like David, they have already sinned. But David repented, and he was forgiven. His beautiful prayer of repentance reveals the proper attitude to take and also shows the loving, merciful nature of God:

Have mercy upon me, O God, according to thy loving-kindness: according unto the multitude of thy tender mercies blot out my transgressions. Wash me throughly from mine iniquity, and cleanse me from my sin. For I acknowl-

*edge my transgressions: and my sin is ever before me. . . .
Behold, thou desirest truth in the inward parts: and in
the hidden part thou shalt make me to know wisdom. Purge
me with hyssop, and I shall be clean: wash me, and I shall
be whiter than snow. Make me to hear joy and gladness;
that the bones which thou hast broken may rejoice. Hide
thy face from my sins, and blot out all mine iniquities.
Create in me a clean heart, O God; and renew a right spirit
within me. Cast me not away from thy presence; and take
not thy holy spirit from me. Restore unto me the joy of
thy salvation; and uphold me with thy free spirit* (Psalm
51:1-3, 6-12).*

*And David said unto Nathan, I have sinned against
the LORD. And Nathan said unto David, the LORD also
hath put away thy sin; thou shalt not die* (II Samuel 12:13).

A person must not give up because of past failures.
Rather it is time to repent, accept the mercy and forgiveness of the Lord, and work towards correcting any
broken trusts. Forgiveness is promised; improved relationships are attainable as the repentant person reaches
out to God and mate.

There is a consolation even in failure if the sinful person obtains restoration. He or she can help others faced
with similar circumstances: "Then will I teach trans-
gressors thy ways: and sinners shall be converted unto
thee" (Psalm 51:13).

Avoiding Job Burnout

Job burnout is a contagious disease for the middle
years. Routine and stress are key culprits. The victim

becomes physically, emotionally, and mentally exhausted. Helplessness and hopelessness prevail, leaving the individual negative about life, people, and job. Certain precautions and corrective measures should be taken to offset these emotions and to develop a renewed outlook.

1. *Take time off from the job.* It is amazing what time away from the office, factory, or truck route can do to renew a worker's emotional and physical condition. There are two ways of taking time off. The first is like letting off steam from a pressure cooker: it is a temporary escape. Examples are an evening fishing trip, a few hours of shopping, or an extra thirty minutes for lunch. A person should take extra time off like this when he or she feels excessively uptight, irritable, or tired. The second way of taking time off is to take a few days or weeks of vacation. Using the analogy of the pressure cooker, it is comparable to turning down the heat.

2. *Exercise regularly.* Exercise should not become a monthly guilt ritual. To receive the proper reward for efforts, some doctors suggest exercising thirty to sixty minutes at least three times a week. A family doctor can prescribe a safe exercise plan.

3. *Enjoy your family.* Most work can be left at the office. A good practice is to use the time it takes to get home from work to change gears: slow down, stop giving orders, breathe deeply and slowly, and think pleasant thoughts.

4. *Establish daily devotions.* Prayer, Bible reading, and Christian music need to be part of our daily life. We can fit our schedule around a daily devotion. We need more than Sunday and Wednesday services to keep us bubbling within and in communion with God.

5. *Laugh a lot.* One husband said, "My wife was having a 'down' day. I remembered just having read a book that suggested laughter as a good therapy for depression. I picked up the book and began to read to her some funnies. It worked! Try it! I readily admit that I read the newspaper comics seven days a week. It's difficult to laugh and be tense at the same time."

6. *Cultivate friendships.* All of us need someone in whom we can confide our fears, hurts, anger, disappointment, and ideas. We will not have many friends like this in a lifetime, but the few we have can help us prevent or escape job burnout.

7. *Change your routine.* Our job may be routine, requiring little mental effort. In fact, it may be downright boring. We can take advantage of the routine to use our minds: to pray, sing, practice a hobby mentally, be creative, prepare a Sunday lesson, memorize Scripture, and so on. Other jobs are the opposite—mentally exhausting. In this case, we can develop a hobby or recreation that gives our mind an enjoyable break.

Preventive Health Care

During midlife, many people experience the gradual breakdown or decline of the body. Someone said, "The knees are the first to go." If health care is overlooked during midlife, health is hard to regain during the latter years. Several areas are critical to good health: a balanced diet, consistent exercise, and proper rest.

Accepting Midlife Graciously

We can enjoy midlife without making it a contest. We must not think we have to outlook, outshoot, outrun, outdo, outsmart, and outtalk everyone around us. One man confessed, "But I feel like the younger generation is tooting their horns and about to pass me up!" They are trying to catch up, not pass. It is a game of life. Before we are tempted to speed up, let us consider that just about the time they have caught us, midlife will catch them. They will slow down, too.

Someone said, "I'd rather burn out than rust out," but someone else noted, "Either way, you're out." We must accept midlife graciously as part of life. This time of life can be very enjoyable. The kids no longer need so much attention. We now have time for personal hobbies, or time to go back to school and obtain an education that has previously eluded us.

At fifty, one minister started college, seeking a degree in education. It has been a fantastic experience for him. His preaching has taken a broader scope. He has a fresh bounce in his step, a bright look at the future. The usual difficulties of life do not get him down. He has focused his attention on a new goal, and those around him have been blessed by it. How different it may have been if he had allowed himself to be overwhelmed by midlife!

It would be good for a couple nearing or in midlife to discuss this chapter together. Afterward, they should pledge to each other to walk the pathway of midlife together with care, watching out for self and each other.

12

This Ole House

*A*ll houses age. The aging process shows no matter how many coats of paint. But properly taken care of, older houses carry an aura of uniqueness and beauty. Likewise we, the inhabitants, are growing older. Our journey can be an adventure, or it can be a nightmare. But it is a journey all of us must take.

Our society is an aging society, and many older people are finding it difficult to cope. Some of the elderly accept society's negative stereotypes of the elderly and become more and more isolated. Many do not adjust well to the process of growing old, while others, reflecting on the past, view themselves as losers. But growing old does not have to be viewed from a negative standpoint. Of course, it has its disadvantages, but many positive things come with age also.

There are two contrasting means of accepting old age: disengagement and activity. In disengagement, the person facing old age succumbs to isolation, loneliness, inactivity, fear, resentment, and unhappiness. By contrast, the person who faces old age with activity, though forced into less favorable conditions, accepts a new role and works toward fulfilling his or her physical, emotional, and spiritual needs. Fulfillment may come from involvement in social services, spiritual growth by way of a renewed commitment to prayer and Bible study, volunteer work in the church or the community, a college course, a hobby, or excelling in grandparenting. The activity model suggests that aging can be successful; successful aging is an acceptance of the passages of life and making the best of them.

Free time, resulting from the children leaving home and from retirement, often breeds loneliness, but the free time should be utilized for productive activities—activities that provide a sense of accomplishment, such as planting a flower garden, reading the Bible through, reading a new book, tackling a new church project, reviving a forsaken outreach program, or shining shoes. These projects can vary from those requiring great effort to those requiring very little effort, depending on the health of the person.

The main goal for the aging person should be to remain active and productive. None of us should be selfish with our time and energy, but we must give sufficient time for the work of the Lord. We must harmonize our control of free time with the teaching of Scripture: "For ye are bought with a price: therefore glorify God in your body, and in your spirit, which are God's" (I Corinthians 6:20). Too many people retire from Christian service when they retire from secular work. Though slowing down is understandable, to quit working for Jesus Christ is detrimental both to the individual and to God's kingdom.

Many aged Bible characters remained productive for the Lord till death. Abraham and Sarah lived out their dream, and God fulfilled His promise to them at ages one hundred and ninety respectively. Moses was eighty years old when God called him to confront Pharaoh and lead the Israelites out of Egypt. He led them for forty years through a wilderness journey. Caleb was eighty-five years old when he entreated Joshua, "Give me this mountain" (Joshua 14:12).

When King David was retirement age, Satan was still fighting him (I Chronicles 21:2). Free time, if spent without regard to our spiritual life and strength, can leave us open to Satan's attacks. Growing old does not exempt us from the Lord's service nor Satan's attack. For the most part, free time should be productive time. Wasted free time leaves us prey to loneliness, depression, self-pity, resentment, and temptation.

How can we avoid these negative emotions? By taking charge of our waking hours, planning activities for the day, week, and year. Some argue, "That takes too much effort," but the effort spent is far less painful than the loneliness, bitterness, and despair that grip the hearts of those who become inactive. Without trying, who knows the happiness that an adventure in older age can bring? Colonel Sanders, founder of Kentucky Fried Chicken, was sixty-six when he decided to share his personal recipe with the world. Today, Kentucky Fried Chicken restaurants operate in fifty-eight countries of the world, serving over one billion meals annually. Likewise, a senior citizen's free time offers opportunity for much service to Jesus Christ. What a revival the church can experience when the retirees give their free time to the work of the Lord!

Loss of a Spouse

Probably the most difficult experience of life is the loss of a spouse; it comes to most during their aging years. This passage of aging offers a hurt that cannot be avoided, only accepted. Though the bereaved spouse longs for that tender touch or that familiar voice to break the silence, it is necessary to give attention to a life that must go on.

Sister Helen Cole wrote with a keen sense of this passage of life:

> Just because you have lost a loved one, you are still alive even though you feel like your life has ended. After many years of happiness in marriage, death strikes, and you wonder, Where do I go from here. I have counseled many people through the years, thinking I knew how they felt.
>
> Not until you have gone through a situation can you really know how others feel. You just think you do. When death or any other grief knocks at your door, only then [do] you [really] know.
>
> The despair, anguish, sorrow, the What-will-I-do? feeling—all of a sudden you realize, I'm not dead, and you feel so alone. You ask, "Why did this happen to me? I have to go on living, so where do I start? I could give up, sit home in a rocking chair, and wait to die; after all, there's nothing to live for anymore." That's the feeling one gets. Oh, but there is [something to live for]! With God's help there is a whole new world out there waiting for what you have to offer. Our life is like a book with many chapters, and each chapter is special in its own right.[1]

The generally accepted stages of grief—denial, anger, bargaining, depression, and acceptance—are passages that the bereaved person must travel through. Two problems can develop: the person may be prodded along too swiftly by well-intentioned but insensitive people (sometimes friends), or the person may get hung up in one or more of the stages.

It is important to realize that these stages and emotions are very normal. A person should not feel guilty for hurting deeply and feeling that there is no reason for going on, but rather should keep on going until the mind and body readjust and say, "I want to go on." If a person keeps on going, given enough time, he or she can adapt to the new role of singleness, although not without pain.

The loss of a spouse means the end of productivity for too many people, who reject the wisdom of affirming, "This too shall pass." Bill Austin, in his superb work, *When God Has Put You on Hold,* observed:

> There are two grave errors that most of us make concerning the interim periods of our lives. First, we live as though they will never happen. . . . The second mistake is living during the interim as though it will last forever. We lose our initiative, creativity, and optimism. We become pedantic, mundane, and pessimistic. The promises of our "false prophets" crash to earth. The rugs of hope are pulled out from under us again and again. We start accepting the unacceptable. Instead of living like human beings with vision and purpose, we live like animals concerned only with today's survival.[2]

197

Christians live with the hope of life eternal with Jesus Christ in heaven. Yet this hope is sometimes shaken when death strikes a loved one. Many people have not come to grips with the biblical concept that everyone except the rapture generation must depart for heaven by way of death. In the quest to have faith in God, by some mental twist some have associated suffering, pain, and sickness with a lack of faith. Thus some view death as the ultimate defeat. But death is not defeat; it is a part of living. Defeat and death are synonymous only for the sinner. Preparation for living includes learning to face death, accepting death's tragic loss, but walking on.

To cope with death, we must recognize that God is ever present. "Yea, though I walk through the valley of the shadow of death, I will fear no evil: for thou art with me; thy rod and thy staff they comfort me" (Psalm 23:4). The valley of death offers much silence, for words are quite inadequate, but silence does not constitute absence. God is there.

Real faith is not rejecting death, but knowing that God is present with us, loving and upholding, even though we do not feel Him. If we keep on going, when the pain has subsided and the fog has lifted we will be surprised at the distance we have covered and the growth we have obtained.

With aging comes a loss of mobility. The adage "the old gray mare ain't what she used to be" is certainly applicable. To some extent mobility can be retained or at least aided by weight reduction, therapy, exercise, and persistence, but much loss of mobility is a part of aging and cannot be prevented or cured. However, much emotional suffering that comes with immobility can be prevented and cured. Loss of mobility does not necessitate a loss of activity, friends, or happiness. With Paul, we must learn to say, "For I have learned, in whatsoever state I am, therewith to be content" (Philippians 4:11). Preceding this verse is a command to dwell on positive thoughts, not negative or discouraging thoughts. "Finally, brethren, whatsoever things are true, whatsoever things are honest, whatsoever things are just, whatsoever things are pure, whatsoever things are lovely, whatsoever things are of good report; if there be any virtue, and if there be any praise, think on these things" (Philippians 4:8).

An inspiring lady, who has been a victim of multiple sclerosis for ten years and who is unable even to turn herself in bed, gave this formula for her enduring happiness through such adversity:

• If your condition cannot be changed, accept it.
• Learn to enjoy the small things—the fragrance of a rose, the pitter-patter of the rain, the stillness of silence—using the senses that remain (hearing is usually the last to go).
• Live and enjoy an hour at a time.
• Talk positively to yourself.
• You still have the right to one of two choices, happiness or sadness. Choose happiness!

Illnesses

Many illnesses typically accompany aging: flu, arthritis, heart disease, poor vision, hearing loss, and so on. They tend not only to slow down a person physically and socially, but they often play havoc with one's faith. Sickness pushes the aged to seek medical attention while faith says to trust God. If the two are seen as incompatible, the result can be additional stress. But we can both trust God and seek the assistance of a physician. Like blind Bartimaeus and the woman with the incurable issue of blood, we must seek Jesus Christ's attention and press into His presence. And when He chooses to perform a miracle in our life, we give Him thanks and praise. Yet to consult doctors who know the cause, prevention, and cure of certain illnesses does not signify a lack of faith, does not insult the Great Physician, for He has allowed these people to have understanding concerning His creation, and He has given them skill. Just as we take our spiritual concerns both to Jesus Christ and a pastor, so we can take our illnesses both to Jesus Christ and a physician without manifesting a lack of spirituality.

Disruption of Home and Awareness of Death

Aging often brings disruption of the home. The old home place that once housed a loving family may no longer be a haven, but a burden: the utility bills are too high for a fixed income, maintenance is too demanding and costly, and stairs are too difficult to climb. A smaller house or apartment can remedy part of the problem, but emotions are tied to the home place. To make a move, especially a forced move, can suggest defeat. But this is not true. Rather, change is part of the process of aging—unpleasant, perhaps, but not defeat.

Disruption of the home signals the inevitable approach of death—but not defeat. Rather, death is a journey to the land of our citizenry. "For our conversation [citizenship] is in heaven; from whence also we look for the Saviour, the Lord Jesus Christ" (Philippians 3:20). Let us face this invitation to heaven with peace, stopping but for a moment to reflect upon and thank those who have given us joy in life, to remind them that we will be waiting to see them again, and to bid them goodbye. Then let us depart into eternal bliss with our Savior, Jesus Christ.

I asked a friend to share her thoughts on aging. Though a member of the aging club, she is not a victim. She asked for a few days to think about it, and in a few days she delivered this poem to me. (Used by permission.)

Growing Old Is Just a Part of Living

'Tis true eyes dim through passing years,
And oft we meet with aging fears.
Weak-kneed, our steps no longer spry,
Though once we led, we now rely.

We no more hear the youthful sound
When joy and laughter did abound.
Take these failures; they are but clay.
We wait for heaven's eternal day.

Old age, hold fast to the Rock unchanging,
Like some bright star beyond planets ranging,
Steadfast and true through journey's length;
So as our days, so is His strength.

We know life's pain is but a span,
And we can't change the Master's plan.
Youth had its day; we shan't compete,
But old-age song is not defeat.

At evening time there shall be light;
Our sun arises unusually bright.
This house holds memories of bygone days,
And sunsets still shed golden rays.

As has been said, "Old age is dark.
But the brightest colors are set
In the sky at twilight and the
Last beams of the day are golden ones."

Zelma Sue Croucher

Notes

Introduction
[1]Fritz Ridenour, "Foreword," in H. Norman Wright, *Communication* (1974).
[2]Lawrence Van Gelder, *New York Times* News Service.
[3]Don Luftig, *Reader's Digest* (1979), 78.

Chapter 1
[1]Joseph (1981).
[2]Findlay (1984).
[3]Townsend (1985).

Chapter 2
[1]Albert Mehrabian (1968).
[2]Paul Tournier, *To Understand Each Other* (John Knox Press, 1967), 8.
[3]Denis Waitley, *Seeds of Greatness* (Old Tappan, N.J.: Fleming H. Revell, 1983), 107.
[4]H. Norman Wright, *Communication* (1974), 157.
[5]Waitley, 183.
[6]"People's Sayso," *Seymour Daily Tribune,* July 10, 1986, 2.
[7]Waitley, 144.
[8]*Seymour Daily Tribune,* July 16, 1986, p. 4.
[9]George Eliot.
[10]Waitley, 144.

Chapter 3
[1]William B. Bradbury, "The Solid Rock."
[2]H. Norman Wright, *Seasons of a Marriage* (Regal Books, 1982), 39.

Chapter 4
[1]*Scott Foresman Advanced Dictionary* (Glenview, Il.: Thorndike/Barnhart, 1979), 1024.
[2]Albert Thomas Howell, *The Lost Wedding Ring* (Hobson Book Press, 1945), 1.
[3]Charlie W. Shedd, *Letters to Philip* (Old Tappan, N.J.: Fleming H. Revell, 1969), 13.

[4]Ibid., 65-66.

[5]Abigail Van Buren, *Chicago Tribune,* 1977.

[6]Rolf Turnbull, quoted in *Leadership,* Fall 1986, 63.

[7]Robert Taylor, *Welcome to the Middle Years* (Acropolis Books, 1976), 153.

[8]Beth Brophy and Gordon Witkin, "Ordinary Millionaires," *Reader's Digest,* Sept. 1986.

Chapter 6

[1]Marilynn Mansfield, News America Syndicate, *The Indianapolis Star,* November 23, 1986.

[2]Monica Dias and Sandy Kinser, "Family," *The Kentucky Post,* December 27, 1986.

[3]Taylor, 159-60.

Chapter 7

[1]Charles R. Swindoll, *Strike the Original Match* (Multnomah Press, 1980), 117.

[2]Tim and Beverly LaHaye, *Spirit-Controlled Family Living* (Old Tappan, N.J.: Fleming H. Revell, 1978), 179.

[3]Gordon McLean, *Let God Manage Your Money* (Grand Rapids: Zondervan, 1972), 14.

[4]*The Thompson Chain Reference Bible* (B. B. Kirkbride Bible Company, 1964).

[5]George M. Bowman, *How to Succeed with Your Money* (Chicago: Moody Press, 1960), 71.

Chapter 9

[1]Dias and Kinser.

[2]Taylor, 116.

[3]Ibid.

Chapter 12

[1]Helen Cole, "Life Doesn't Have to End, You Can Love Again," *Christian Educator* UPCI General Sunday School Division, Fall 1989.

[2]Bill Austin, *When God Has Put You on Hold* (Wheaton, Il.: Tyndale House Publishers, 1986), 117.